PIMPS

IN THE PULPIT

Herbert Brown

An In Step Publishing Book

For information regarding permission, write to:

In Step Publishing, P.O. Box 307, Skippers, VA 23879

herbert.brown1@verizon.net Email Address.

ISBN 0-9634738-3-2

Copyright @ 1998-2008 by In Step Publishing

All rights reserved. Published by In Step Publishing

Editing, graphic layout and cover illustration

by Souleye – soulcis@autoreverseweb.com

Printed in the U.S.A

First In Step Publishing, May 1999

Updated and Revised In Step Publishing, June 2008

Author's Note:

As a result of the tremendous feedback that I got from so many readers of the first edition of *"Pimps in the Pulpit"*, I decided to add a glossary to this edition. I received countless comments like: "I enjoyed your book, but some of the words were a little difficult."... "Your book was great, but I had to have a dictionary in order to understand it."... "Your book was truly wonderful, but I certainly wished that you hadn't laid the big words on so thick." These are but a few of the great comments that I've received about the book and now I've tried my best to address them. So this is why I've added the glossary, to bring a bit more clarity and understanding to the message.

I did not intentionally use so many of these (big words) just for the sake of trying to sound smart or sophisticated, the fact of the matter is, that in order for me to adequately address this subject, I had to use a number of terms and concepts from the social sciences: Political Science, History, Psychology, Religion, Sociology, and Economics. I have also added a table of contents to this edition along with more chapters of which I hope, will broaden and deepen the scope of the original message. I cannot find words powerful enough to express my deep appreciation for your tremendous support of the first edition of *"Pimps in the Pulpit"*, however, I dare not take credit for anything good between the pages of that book, or even this book, because I know that I'm just a messenger, the true credit, honor, and all praise belong to Yahweh the Most High, that Divine Architect of all good, just, righteous, and eternal things.

Herbert E. Brown graduated from the Virginia School at Hampton Virginia for the Deaf and Blind in 1975. He graduated from the Virginia State College with a Bachelor's Degree in Political Science and a Minor in Psychology in 1978. Next he earned a Master's Degree in Political Science from the Ohio State University in 1979, and earned another Bachelor's Degree in Social Studies in 1980. Mr. Brown has worked as a Substitute Teacher for the Franklin County Public Schools in Columbus, Ohio, and a regular teacher for Sonshine Christian Academy also in Columbus. He has been a Snack bar and Cafeteria Manager with the state of Ohio's Business Enterprise Program. He currently works as an Independent Living Advocate with Insight Enterprises, Inc., a Center for Independent Living located in Hampton, Virginia. Mr. Brown self-published *"Blood or Justice"* a young adult fiction novel in 1993. He has published two children's books: *"The Howling Night"*, 1998 and *"Bennie the Rapper"*, 1999.

CONTENTS

FOREWORD

TO THE BLACK CHURCH IN AMERICA

The crucible of the Black church has been unalterably ruptured by Herbert E. Brown in his new book, The Black Church in America. His effusive, jackhammer style essay has unleashed a torrent of criticism on this once venerable institution which, like the sped arrow, is not easily recovered or ignored. The hot ore of his scathing look at the African-American religious institution of overwhelming choice blisters the reader's blissful comfort level with searing intensity. Mr. Brown's personal style departs from the sedate, dispassionate offerings of previous authors critically examining the establishment and evolution of this powerful, wealthy and influential, quasi-religious community.

Departing with vigor from the restraints of such writers as C. Eric Lincoln and Lawrence H. Mamiya's, The Black Church in the African American Experience, and Carter G. Woodson's seminal work, A History of the Black Church, Herbert E. Brown's personal essay is unique in its conception in that its unbridled criticism and analysis make no pretense of academic historiography or "objective" scientific ologies imposed on predecessors by their caution. His work is so suffused with primal passion and unadulterated indignation that it will surely be included in a separate category of Phillip Lopate's next edition of The Art of the Personal Essay. A son of Virginia, not unlike the most venerated American icon of the same soil, Thomas Jefferson, Mr. Brown shares the same philosophical and ideological iconoclasm regarding the conditions of the Christian church in America. While Jefferson was so driven by his vision that he wrote extensively on the subject and produced what is often referred to as the "Jefferson Bible,"

H.E. Brown has focused his attention on the black Christian church in its degraded contemporary form. The need for a continuing examination of the church's status consequences, and influence is made exquisitely clear as Brown takes a sledge-hammer to it as befitting a primary civilizing institution that is self-evidently do Mig the opposite. By design and with good intent, the approach and conception is that of unerring criticism and unencumbered prescient analysis. Among its most unique features is the novel, entertaining, yet serious description of three types of preachers who pervade the pulpit of the black church: the pimp, the punk and pusher. This bare-knuckle personality profile of church leadership types will surely ring true to some, outrage others and cause spiritual pain to the spiritually vulnerable. Mr. Brown's litany of the failures of the black church cuts across the intellectual disciplines of education, economics, sociology, psychology, history and theology. He excoriates with particular unrepentant candor the ugliness in the Black Church caused by the unexpurgated fealty and Siamese-like attachment to the dominant white church its historically oppressive theology and unwholesome theologians.

As if oblivious to the inherent racism that permeates all of America's civilizing institutions formed under western's imperialism, the black church has become less than an empty shell devoid of truth and righteousness; it has become a demonic temple of spir-

8

itual death, fueling a life-threatening erosion of black people in all areas of human existence. Mr. Brown has captured the essence of the personal essay in this book, an essential characteristic of which is described by Phillip Lopate* in the following quotation: "It is often the case that personal essayists intentionally go against the grain of popular opinion. They raise the ante, as it were, making it more difficult for the reader to identify frictionlessly with the writer. The need to assert a quite specific temperament frequently leads the essayist into playing the curmudgeon, for there is no quicker way to demonstrate idiosyncrasy and independence that to stand a platitude on its head, to show a prickly opposition to what the rest of humanity views as patently wholesome of the find merits in what the community regards as loathsome."

Herbert Elliot Brown has encircled the Black Church and has thereby placed it in a position of needing to reform itself in order to extricate itself from the throes of repugnance and putridity. And, while so doing, he has written in a manner in pristine congruence with the essayist's charge as proffered by Lopate below: "The essayist attempts to surround a something – a subject, a mood, a problematic irritation-by coming at it from all angles, wheeling and diving like a hawk, each seemingly digressive spiral actually taking us closer to the heart of the matter. In a well-wrought essay, while the search appears to be widening, even losing its way, it is actually eliminating false hypotheses, narrowing its emotional target and zeroing in on it."

Dr, James A. Fox, University of the District of Columbia, November 1998

ACKNOWLEDGEMENT

First, I give Yahweh the praise, the glory, and the honor for giving me the inspiration, elucidation, and determination to start, and finish this book. Secondly, I extend my heart-felt gratitude to Miss Yvonne Booker, Miss Cindy Peoples, Miss Kym Jackson, Mrs. Shirley Little, and my wife, Mrs. Barbara Cunningham-Brown whom so faithfully assisted me with the typing and research of this book. Also, I extend my sincerest appreciation to Dr. James Fox, Mr. Souleye Cisse, and Miss Sharon Shula for their invaluable assistance with the editing and preparation of this book. Finally, I want to thank all of my dear relatives and friends who are too numerous to mention here, but whose prayers, moral support, and encouragement have sustained me over the years.

I dedicate this book to the precious memory of my late mother, Mary Etta Brown, father, Herbert E. Brown Senior, brother, Larry D. Brown, and first cousin, James A. Epps. I am looking forward to seeing them again some day in that place where we shall never grow old. I'm talking about that beautiful and eternal place beyond the River Jordan, where pain will have no power, and death, no dominion. Yes, I'm talking about the New Jerusalem, where we'll all gather as saints and friends and Sabbath will have no end, where there will be no more goodbyes and Yahweh the Most High, Himself, will wipe all tears from our eyes.

PIMPS IN THE PULPIT

The truth is often like good medicine: bitter to taste and hard to swallow

CHAPTER 1

The African-American Church as an Institution

The African-American church has stood as a spiritual lighthouse with its bright beacon guiding African-Americans across the bitter centuries of slavery. It has also been the great spiritual reservoir from which African-Americans have drawn celestial power that has supported and sustained them while they wandered for generations in the dark wilderness of hopelessness, powerlessness, and utter despair. They were searching for that promised freedom that eluded them for a century after the close of the Civil War. The African-American church was born out of the desperate longing of these people in bondage and shaped by the spiritually grinding forces of that bondage. This was that peculiar institution which designated Africans as the cursed children of Ham, as beasts of burden, to be bought and sold like other domesticated farm animals. These sons and daughters of Africa, in the eyes of Europeans, were on the evolutionary scale somewhere between man and beast. They were to be used as drawers of water and hewers of wood and to faithfully serve their masters with gladness. In the process, they would be raised to an

11

acceptable level of civilization by association with their technologically developed and culturally refined, Christian masters. So out of the ruthless brutality of bondage, the slaves cried out to the God of their masters. This spiritual contact enabled them to endure their plight. So the slaves embraced this God and made him their own.

Even the few free Africans living in North America found themselves existing in a kind of perennial slavery. They were all but totally locked out of every aspect of American life. After finding themselves unwelcome and unwanted in the white church denominations, these freed men organized their own churches. Facing the same oppression and brutal domination as their slave countryman, the church was their only sanctuary from a hostile white world. It was one of the few places where they could feel accepted and appreciated. Inside its consecrated walls they could be spiritually rejuvenated, after enduring the relentless hostility of white society. In their holy tabernacle, they could consecrate themselves in God's love and draw solace from the belief that they were as valuable in his eyes as the rest of humanity. In His word He declared that he had sacrificed his son in hope to save all men from their sin. John, 3:16. "For God so loved the world that he gave his only begotten son and who so ever believeth in him shall not perish, but have ever lasting life." The church was the wellspring of spiritual sustenance which enabled African-Americans to survive and even thrive in a land where they were despised, reviled and rejected, simply because of who and what they were.

12

Many historians believe that the African slaves embraced Protestant denominations largely because the religious rituals practiced by these groups were very similar to their native African religions. Therefore, the various Protestant denominations were adopted and adapted by Africans who were brought to North America in the hulls of slave ships. From the outset, many slave owners saw the benefit in introducing their slaves to Christianity because of its tenants of unquestioned obedience and the immeasurable rewards for the faithful in the after life. These masters saw the Christian religion as a tool that could make their job easier in controlling their bondsmen. They realized the potential for even greater psychological control in those ideals of faithfulness, obedience, and total submission to the ordained authority that (Christianity) required of its believers.

Therefore the slave masters used the religion as a stupendously powerful psychological tool for handling the slave. Many a cunning slave owner used the slaves fear and admonition of God and his native longing to rest in the bosom of Abraham after his miserable sojourn down on earth to bind him tighter to his master, and make him a more complete slave. The African-American preacher has been reviled, excoriated, and vilified for his complicity in this awful conspiracy, since he was the natural instrument through which the slave master worked his wicket magic on the rest. Conversely there were a few notable exceptions, like Net Turner, Denmark Vesey, and Gabriel Prosser, who were all slave preachers, but who actually tried to use their position and influence to free their

13

countrymen. However, most slave preachers were no more than servile lackeys for their masters.

Yet, there have been many other African-American members of the clergy, since slavery, who have been in the forefront of the African-American's relentless struggle for political and social rights and economic freedom. In the wake of the civil war and in the shadow of Jim Crow, there was *Plessey vs. Ferguson*, the infamous U.S. Supreme Court's decision of 1896 which imposed a legal system of apartheid on American society. The African-American church has been the only real sanctuary for the African self. Consequently, it has been the only bulwark against the total spiritual and psychological annihilation of that African self in hostile white America. The African-American church has spawned, nurtured, and cultivated the greatest number of African-American leaders.

Nevertheless, it has not been a monolith in its philosophical orientation with regards to the scope, depth and severity of the problems confronting African-Americans, nor has the African-American church been single minded or unified in its approach to the solutions of these problems. On the contrary, there has historically been, and continues to be much fragmentation and factionalism in the African-American church. This has greatly diminished its ability to deal with the vast array of political, social, and economic problems impacting the lives of African-Americans. It is precisely this paradox, that I intend to examine, and this great irony that I intend to investigate. While the African-American church has been a liberator of the African-American's spirit, it has also been the enslaver of his mind. As it has inspired, encouraged and impelled the African-American's spirit to majestic heights in the cosmology of sanctimony, it has simultaneously been used as a tool of psychological control and mental docility. Therefore, the church has been both a blessing and a curse. So, it is in this context that I intend to examine its influence on the African-American community through its main proponents, African-American preachers.

The black church is the only cultural institution in America that is, by and large, controlled by the African-American Community. It is the only institution whose goals and objectives can be set forth virtually independent of the larger white society. Also, it is the only cultural institution in the African-American community that wields such a powerful influence in the lives of the great majority of black folk. However, this power has been historically, and remains for the most part, to be merely potential. This great potential power of the black church has never been really organized and activated in the fullness of its force to solve the political, social, and economic problems of the community. Yes, we have seen hint of this great potential power which galvanized African Americans in the civil rights movement under the leadership of Reverend Doctor Martin Luther King Jr..

King's movement nurtured, supported and sustained by the church was able to focus the eyes of the world on America and her great hypocrisy. She was finally shamed into grudgingly granting African-Americans their citizenship rights that the Constitution had guaranteed them over a century earlier. With his philosophy of non-violence and direct action, King was able to dramatize the injustice and hypocrisy of American society and prick the conscience of decent people everywhere. This resulted- in a global out pouring of righteous indignation, against the rank hypocrisy of a nation who proclaimed itself to the world to be the standard bearer of freedom while it held 15 percent of its population in perennial slavery.

When King was assassinated on April 4, 1968, the movement that he had led splintered into a number of factions, leaving none of them nowhere near as strong as the original organization. Since the death of Martin Luther King Jr. and the subsequent decline of the civil rights movement, the African-American church has, for the most part, languished in petty self-indulgence while the social and economic problems affecting the community have grown steadily worse. The African-American church seems to have become far more pre-occupied and self-absorbed with dancing, singing, preaching, and praying, behind its stain glass windows and consecrated walls, than developing, building, and supporting positive social and economic structures in the community. It seems to be far too preoccupied with the misguided notion of, "Pie in the sky, after you die," than with providing education, jobs, and creating economic opportunities for community self-determination, while one is living in the, "Here and now". The African-American church has been a great paradox, a blessing and a curse, a liberator, and, an enslaver, a talisman and a tool and thus it remains one of the great ironies of African-American life.

The black church stands alone as the only institution in the African-American community that has historically enjoyed the highest level of social approval and financial support from the community. The church represents the greatest number of African-Americans coming together on a regular basis. It is also the only institution in the African-American community which has historically enjoyed and continues to enjoy such a high level of financial support from the community. However, I contend that it has been a miserable steward over the finances of its parishioners. Even the church associations and organizations among the various denominations have given pitifully little account of the millions of dollars that they have taken in over the years. Furthermore, these same church organizations and associations regularly engage in meticulous planning to secure fine hotels for lavish conventions and convocations where they spend millions of dollars every year with major white hotel chains. Yet, they don't seem to have the time or inclination to even try to articulate an economic or social agenda for the very people that they claim to represent.

The black church as a whole, seems far more interested in spending the money of its parishioners on ever more opulent edifices, and on the insatiable greed of self-indulgent preachers, than truly investing in any serious economic development of the community. Far too many individual churches are caught up in a frantic determination to outdo one another, in their gaudy extravagance with the building of ever larger, more opulent, and more expensive places of worship. As a result, they have all but totally neglected the real economic and social needs of the very people that they profess to serve. This tragic reality can be blamed squarely on the heads of the African-American clergy.

Too many black preachers seem to be far more concerned with self-magnanimity, ego-tripping, and the internal affairs of their particular churches than in the general welfare of the community. They tend to have a pitifully myopic view of reality. For example, they tend to see their own particular church bodies as the only thing really worthy of their efforts and attention. Furthermore they tend to see their own churches as the most righteous and authentic practice of Christianity. Consequently, this view adds to their attitude of self-righteousness and religious snobbery. Therefore, these distorted attitudes and egotistical machinations so pervasive among the black clergy, are the very forces which operate to prohibit constructive inter, and intra-church cooperation. As a result, the various churches become islands of gelded hope surrounded by decay and despair. The preachers are lords of their own little fiefdoms; proud, preening, prancing roosters, intoxicated with an exaggerated sense of their own self-worth and the power that they hold over the lives of their flocks. Therefore, it is the African-American preacher, who has been the guiding force of the church and consequently the preacher has been either victim, or villain, tool or fool, and prophetic or pathetic in the extremely critical role as spiritual leader of the African-American community.

CHAPTER 2

The Pimp Preacher

In this chapter and in two succeeding chapters, I am going to examine three personality types that I have observed among African-American preachers. The various traits that I intend to discuss are not exclusive to African-American preachers. On the contrary, these extremely negative character traits can be found in every racial and ethnic group in Christendom. However, for the purposes of this book, African-American preachers are the focus of my concern.

First of all, I am going to examine the preacher personality that I refer to as the "Pimp Preacher". The pimp preacher has three main character traits that are clearly recognizable to the most casual observer. First, he has an over arching need to drain the congregation of every dime that he can possibly get. Secondly, there is an almost psychotic need for gaudy ostentation and a frantic pursuit of high elegant living. Then there is the need to use the church to acquire a measure of political power. However, even though the church is used to establish a base of political power, this power is never actually used for the benefit of the congregation or black community at large. It is primarily used to further enrich the pimp preacher and his cronies. Moreover, this political power may sometimes even be used to the detriment of the church and community when it suits the pimp preacher's personal agenda or self-aggrandizing purpose. This individual is first and fore most concerned with money and his mind is constantly preoccupied with how to get more of it. He is constantly dreaming and scheming up ways in which he can more efficiently fleece his flock. He is usually the mastermind behind every kind of bake sale, banquet, luncheon, musical program, and any other church auxiliary function that is designed to raise money. This type of preacher often tailors his or her every message from the pulpit to fit the overriding effort to get more money. He often cultivates close relationships with those members who are inclined to give largely and regularly. He may lavish praise and affection on those who give large amounts of money to the church to the point where he becomes obsequious and even unctuous in his sycophantic fawning over those church "Big shots".

Conversely, he will hardly notice those who are not so loose with the purse strings or those, who because of their economic circumstances are not able to feed the church coffers to such an extent. This pimp preacher also makes no bones about the fact that he believes that the members should give until it hurts. This pimp has no shame in his merciless demands for more money from the congregation. For if the collection plate does not yield what he expects during the first round of giving in a particular service, he will suspend any further worship activities and re-circulate the collection plate until it is filled with the amount of money that he wants. He is extremely skilled at using the Bible, especially appealing to fear and guilt in his ruthless efforts to coerce the flock into making a greater sacrifice by forking over more and more of their meager income. He is most adept at using fear and guilt in a determined effort to extract the last dime, usually from those who can least afford to give it. "Will a man rob God?" "Yes, you can rob god in your tithes and offerings. What if god was as stingy with us as we are with him? We've got to realize, that you must first plant the seed before you can hope to get a harvest, Christian friends." "God loves a cheerful giver." "The Bible says, where a man's treasure is, that's where his heart is." He often couches his appeal for money in terms that make members feel extremely guilty if they don't fork over all of their meager means. This individual is very skilled in manipulating people's psychological and spiritual need or desire to please their God by the insinuation of fear and guilt. "You must sew the seed of faith, if you want to reap the harvest." "You must cast your bred upon the water, and it will be returned to you greatly multiplied. "Give and God will give to you, shaken up, pressed down, and running over." These are some of the scriptures, and half scriptures that I have often heard used over and over again to probe and prod people who could least afford it, to indeed give until it definitely hurt.

Another trait of this type of individual is the mindless obsession with fine clothes and expensive cars. The pimp preacher just as his counterpart on the street is quite consumed with gaudy ostentation. He stimulates, cultivates, and promotes the natural desire of most African-American church members to see their preachers looking good and riding in quintessential style. Therefore, he argues that he is an extension of them. For the most part, his members

21

must start to perceive of him as just that, an extension of themselves. As a result, they live vicariously through him, and are careful to see that he rides in the finest cars, wears the finest clothes, and lives in the finest home. This attitude of keeping their preachers dressed in the most elegant finery and riding in quintessential style, is quite pervasive throughout the African-American church. The competition between church congregations to elevate and maintain their preachers in an exaggerated height of style and elegance has created a gaudy aristocracy among the black clergy. So the pimp preacher's obsession is to be numbered among this class of the beautiful, the class of style, elegance, and comfort. This means that he has truly arrived. So the pimp preacher lives in regal splendor off the sweat, blood, and the hard earned money of his parishioners. Unfortunately, the great majority of black parishioners are proud of their effort to support and sustain their preachers in this way, because again, they live vicariously through him and see him as an idealized representation of themselves. However, the real tragedy of it all is that the money being lavished on the preacher to create and maintain his gaudy life style of elegance and ease is sorely needed to help the needy right there in his own congregation.

Another pronounced trait of the pimp preacher worth mentioning here is his ability to ingratiate himself to the flock to the point where they are almost irrational in their affection for him. The pimp on the street is often able to accomplish this same effect on his prostitutes by lavishing upon them, his pretense of genuine affection. So he accomplishes this by supplying them with cheap gifts, drugs, a place to stay, and protection. As a result, the unfortunate prostitute becomes psychologically dependent on the pimp and will work hard and long to keep the money coming in for him. Similarly the pimp preacher operates in much the same way. He ingratiates himself to his members through the false pretense of his concern for their souls. He may visit them in their homes or in the hospital when they happen to be ill. Moreover, he may help them with some legal, financial, or family problem.

These are all things which will certainly ingratiate and endear the preacher to most of his members and then they will reward him lavishly, with their money and undying affection. The pimp preacher, just as the street pimp, is careful to cultivate and maintain this relationship of psychological dependency and milk it for all that it is worth. Most pimp preachers have managed to cultivate and enhance this sycophantic relationship to a point where if they are accused, and even found guilty of some serious sin, they are quickly forgiven by their congregations. Ironically, they often emerge from the ordeal even stronger and more influential than they were before. In a deeper examination of the dynamics of the pimp prostitute relationship, one cannot escape the conclusion that the street pimp is a great deal more faithful to his role of supplying drugs, shelter, and protection to his prostitutes, than the pimp preacher has ever been in his role as spiritual leader and custodian of the social welfare of his flock. In this light, the street pimp is far more noble a figure, in that he at least makes good on his promise. Conversely, the pimp preacher promises much and delivers very little in any significant way to the congregation that supports and sustains him in his lavish lifestyle.

A former deacon of a large church located in Columbus Ohio told me the following story which poignantly underscores my description of the classic pimp preacher. There was a business meeting among the deacons and the preacher. The purpose of this meeting, which had been called by the preacher, was to discuss the preacher's upcoming trip to the Holy Land. The deacon related to me that the tension in the room was so thick that you could have cut it with a knife. He said that when the preacher finally opened the meeting, he and every one else present could see that their pastor was visibly annoyed when he brought up the matter of his pending trip. He glared around the room from face to face as each of the deacon's eyes dropped miles into the floor when the preacher's flinty gaze locked with their own. He went on to explain how the one thousand dollars in spending money allotted for him and the additional thousand allotted for his wife was nowhere near enough for such a trip.

The fact that the church was already paying him a handsome salary and providing him with a church supported home, and had already paid all of the travel and hotel accommodations for this trip, didn't seem to matter at all to him. This pimp preacher still had the unmitigated gall to stand there and almost demand that the deacon board double the two thousand dollars initially allotted for he and his wife. When this pimp preacher had finally finished his pathetic appeal which the deacon felt was more couched in tones of a demand than a request, he just stood there glaring at the deacons as if they had totally failed to grasp the compelling conclusion of his courtroom-like summation. He'd rattled on for nearly an hour, telling them how deeply he was in debt, and how awfully wrong they would be to deny his absurd demand for more money. The room fell silent for a long time.

The Storyteller said he just sat there and watched those grown men cowering beneath the weight of their pastor's baleful stare. Then suddenly he said that a sickening feeling came over him, because he simply couldn't believe what he was hearing. He said that he could not believe that this man was standing before them asking them for more money and was actually expecting to get it. He said that the more he turned this over in his mind, he quickly realized why he was feeling sick and the sickening feeling quickly melted into rage which made his blood boil. "My God, Pastor," he said, fighting to control his seething disgust, "the church has already paid all of your travel expenses." "We felt that the thousand dollars a piece for you and your wife would be more than enough, taken with what we already pay you in salary." He said that he then watched the preacher's eyes grow cold with disdain as his lips curl into a hateful sneer, but still he continued. When he looked around at the fellow deacons to gauge their reaction, he noticed that they all seemed to breathe a collective sigh of relief. He had dared to say, what they, in their hearts, had really wanted to say, but they just didn't have the courage to stand up to this brazen pimp. So when he'd spoken up against this ridiculous idea, the pimp preacher seemed to focus his unmasked hostility directly on him. Yet and still he continued. "Pastor," he said plaintively, "there are people right here in this congregation who can't even hardly pay their rent and buy food for their children.

The church needs to be doing more to help these folks! Now here we are, sitting here talking about giving you more money to spend on a vacation." He said that as he explained these well known facts about some members of the congregation, he noticed that the Pimp's cold eyes were still glaring at him, but now there was a clear glint of disappointment in them, because he knew that the answer to his ridiculous request would be an unequivocal no. Especially, after this individual had concluded his case against the idea, poignantly spelling out the true needs of many of the less fortunate members right there in their congregation and balancing them against the naked greed of this arrogant pimp preacher. The deacon knew, and they all knew, that to submit to their pastors absurdly selfish request would be an abomination before God. Especially, in light of the pervasive lack among many of the members, right there in the congregation, of the basic necessities of life. Nevertheless, this same pimp preacher would later use his power to exact revenge on this deacon who had had the audacity to challenge him, by refusing to ordain him into the priesthood. This individual was eventually ordained and is now pastor of a church. Ironically, his wife elected to stay behind and, to this day, remains a staunch supporter and very active member of this pimp preacher's congregation.

As pathetic as this is, I am not surprised. Why? Because pimp preachers, like their counterparts in the streets, are usually able to exercise far more control

26

over women than they can over men. I have experienced this sinister phenomenon in my own personal life. Once during my marriage, my former wife and I were attending a charismatic holiness church. This was a church where the pastor wielded, what I saw as an unhealthy influence, over many of his female members, and my former wife was one of them. Needless to say, this had a very deleterious effect on our marriage. However, unable to break the pastor's influence over my wife, all I could do was to become angry and resentful like many other men I knew who felt like their wives were far more willing to listen to, and be more obedient to their pastors than they were to their husbands. I also was to learn later that I was not the only man in that particular congregation who was forced to deal with this diabolical phenomenon. I call it, the barnyard pimp syndrome. Why? Because it is the situation where the pastor of a church totally dominates the lives and affairs of his members much like the rooster dominates the affairs of the barnyard. Just like the rooster, proud, preening, pompous, and arrogant, tolerates no dissension under his dominion, the pimp preacher tolerates no dissension in his church. So even the men have to acquiesce and submit to his domination or leave the church. Therefore, men who are just unable to allow themselves, to be so thoroughly dominated by another man, will ultimately leave these types of churches. However more often than not, their wives will opt to stay behind.

This same preacher, I was told, had direct access to another church member's bank account through the man's wife. His wife was allowing this preacher to write checks on their bank account. At first the individual said that he did not complain because the preacher had claimed that he was buying things for the church. However when the man decided to investigate and found that many of the items that the preacher claimed that he was buying for the church were unaccounted for, he confronted the preacher. This pimp became indignant and told him that he did not have to give any account to him for anything, the fact that he was drawing money from this man's bank account notwithstanding. So when the man tried to put his foot down and cut off this unnatural preacher privilege, his own wife rose up in the preacher's defense and staunchly refused to cut off this pimp preacher's access to their bank account. This pathetic situation, the man lamented, almost caused the break up of his marriage before it was finally effectively dealt with. I also learned of other examples just as pathetic but too numerous to mention in my particular church and others, where the preachers held far too much influence over the women in the congregation, even married women. As a result of this unnatural preacher influence many of the men felt impotent, alienated, and distant from their own wives. These husbands naturally resented the fact that their spouses were more inclined to listen to, and obey the preacher before they would them. Again, I submit that this is an unnatural, an unhealthy, and a perverse relationship that is based on a sycophantic loyalty and blind obedience to one's pastor. Moreover, it warrants a far more thorough investigation and analysis than I am able to give here.

Finally, I also learned of the countless other stories where wives had opted to attend a different church than their husbands. On the surface this may not seem like a serious matter. However when one is conversant with the actual functioning of churches even within the same denomination, the matter takes on an ominous quality. Why? Because most preachers tend to view the particular church where they happen to pastor as their own personal domain. Consequently, they see it as the mirror reflection of their own views, rightly or wrongly. Furthermore, they tend to view the church that they pastor as an extension of themselves. Therefore, nothing but their own particular brand of the gospel is preached and practiced in that particular church. This is why there are so many deep and vast differences in interpretation, style, and context in the way that the gospel is taught by preachers supposedly using the same Bible. Moreover, this is usually the situation even within the same Christian denomination. Consequently, it is now clear and logical to see how the incidence of man and wife attending two different churches could create and promote tremendous conflict in a marriage over the most basic values and beliefs concerning the institution of marriage and the family. For this absurd notion of the gospel according to the particular pastor of a particular church is the primary reason why there is so much strife, confusion, and conflict not only in families, but also among Christians in general.

Now, back to my discussion of the pimp preacher and his methods of exploitation of his flock. The third and perhaps most ominous trait of the pimp preacher is that of using the church to establish his own personal political power base. This could be an admirable ability, if the leader had the interest of the church faithful at heart. However, it becomes something ugly and perverse when we observe how pimp preachers actually use the church as a power base only to establish political power for themselves.

For example, once he has used the church as a springboard for the accomplishment of his political aspirations, he is finished with it in terms of using the political clout that he has obtained at the expense of the church to do anything concrete or constructive for his parishioners. In other words, once attaining some measure of political success, he will do absolutely nothing for the community whose votes made his political success possible. Furthermore, the pimp preacher has used the church as a power base from which to bargain away parishioners votes for political favors from the white power elite downtown. He thinks nothing at all of sacrificing the needs and interest of his own people for a seat on some board or commission down town. He is also a prostitute for the white power elite when it needs someone to support a bond issue or referendum which may not be in the interest of the black community.

The pimp preacher is always ready and willing to step up, on behalf of his white benefactors, and stamp his black face on the issue. Then he will work day and night and even use his sham religion in order to sell it to the black community. This unconscionable duplicity is being done by black preachers and other black politicians every day across America. These lowlife house Negroes have so refined their scurvy methods of selling out their own people that they have made it an insidious art. As I have fore stated, the pimp preacher not only exploits his own church but he stoops even lower than the street pimp, by letting others, who are just as unscrupulous and immoral, come in and fleece his flock too. A good friend of mine who attends a large church in Columbus, Ohio, told me a story about how a large bank in the city made an arrangement with his church to facilitate church members efforts in securing home mortgage loans. On its face, this looked like an outstanding gesture on the part of the bank. However, as I have learned over the years, one must look at a thing deeper than the surface, if there is to be any true understanding of it. A deeper investigation of this arrangement between his church and the bank revealed that there was a financial limit placed on these mortgages by this bank and anything over that amount, it refused to underwrite.

Furthermore, the bank established a specific geographical area of the city from which the homes had to be purchased. My friend told me that there was much joy and jubilation among the church leaders and members alike about their relationship with the bank. The church members would often boast that they were one of the only black churches in the city with such a fantastic relationship with a major bank. My friend said that, initially he thought that it was a good thing. About six months after this historic relationship had been established with this bank, my friend, who owns a small business, said that he went to this same bank trying to get a five thousand dollar business loan. He said that he had always had excellent credit and had been in business for 24 years, however, this same bank that had been so willing to extend mortgage loans to the church members would

31

not extend him a five thousand dollar business loan. Needless to say, he was very disappointed but as he left the bank empty handed and stepped out on to the street a revelation exploded in his brain like a flash of lightening. The same bank that was so willing to cozy up with his church which has a very large congregation, under the pretext of making it easier for them to get mortgage loans, was really not acting in the best interest of the church folk at all. The leaders of this bank had simply identified a consumer market and gone after it. This was strictly a business decision which no doubt was beneficial to the bank in purely economic terms.

Therefore, the bank's decision to exploit this economic market had little or nothing whatsoever, to do with corporate character, or the bank's concern for the welfare of the black community. He deduced, that it was far more profitable for the bank to extend a mortgage loan to African-Americans, than to extend a business loan. Under the interest structure and payment terms of a standard thirty-year mortgage, the initial purchase price of the average home would actually be paid three or four times, by the time the mortgage loan is paid in full. This arrangement represents tremendous profits for the bank. On the other hand, a small business loan would not yield such enormous profits. Furthermore, it would raise the specter of African-American economic independence if the business were even marginally successful. Therefore, he realized that the bank was not interested in the church congregation at all, except when the situation was extremely profitable for it to do so. My friend went on to say how he had discussed his ordeal concerning the bank with the church leaders, but outside of their slack-jawed mouthing of their hollow sympathy nothing was done. He said that he was not surprised in the least at the response of those church leaders, because to do nothing was the only logical and predictable alternative that they could offer. This kind of weak-kneed, lily-livered, hat-in-hand pimp preacher leadership has no heart for really doing what's right and no genuine love for the faithful. If this were not the case, then these pimp preachers would not be so ready and willing to conspire with forces outside of the African-American community to exploit and oppress their own people.

In the final analysis, those good and decent people in these congregations must take a stand. They must stand up for what they say that they believe, and declare that any man who comes preaching anything other than the true gospel of Jesus Christ, let him be accursed. *Galatians 1:6-10.* "But though we, or an angel from heaven, preach any other gospel unto you than that which we have preached unto you, let him be accursed." They must demand quality leaders who are truly called by God and who are equipped and qualified by Him to be a true shepherd of His flock. How can the honest and decent people in the congregation do this? First, they must study the word of God for themselves; the Bible commands it. *II Timothy 2:15*, "Study to show thyself approved unto God, a workman that needed not to be ashamed, rightly dividing the word of truth". Verse 16, "But shun profane and vain babbling, for they will increase unto more ungodliness." Then they must pray and look only to Jesus Christ as their example for living the true Christian life. For Jesus said in *John 15: 5-7*, "I am the vine, ye are the branches. He that abideth in me, and I in him, the same bringeth forth much fruit: for without me ye can do nothing. If ye abide in me, and my word abide in you, ye shall ask what you will, and it shall be done unto you." For the most part, the low quality of leaders, which are little, more than parasites now running the African-American church are about what the parishioners who support them deserve. When good and righteous people fail to stand up against these pimp preachers, the church becomes little more than a hapless flock to be fleeced, used, and exploited by the very leadership supposedly, ordained by God, to lead and protect it. The Bible also commands Christians to watch and pray: to draw nigh to God and he will draw nigh to you. *James 4:8*, "Draw nigh to God, and He will draw nigh to you. Cleanse your hands, ye sinners; and purify your hearts, ye double minded." Jesus declares that, anyone who diligently seeks him will surely find Him. Jesus asserts, "Behold, I stand at the door and knock, he who opens his heart, I will come in and sup with him and he with me." *Rev. 3:20-23*. Those who are willing to except Him as their personal Lord and Savior, and be baptized, He has promised to give them a comforter who will lead them into all righteousness. *John 14:26*. People must try the spirit by the spirit. If God is not leading your preacher, his actions, and more importantly, the Holy Spirit will reveal that to you.

There are many people who sit cowardly and closed mouthed under these infamous pimp preachers, watching them ruthlessly exploit the church body and can't find the backbone to raise the feeblest protest. Any preacher who refuses to address the basic and natural physical needs of the church congregation can, in no way, be trusted to address its spiritual needs. These pimp preachers must be removed if the spiritual, social, and economic health of the church is ever to be realized. Any church leader who does not recognized the extremely critical need for community development and black self-determination and cannot understand and appreciate that the African-American church must be in the forefront of these efforts is simply out of touch with the reality of the community. There can be no truc spiritual leader in the African-American church who does not feel compelled to find a way to bring the economic power and moral authority of the church to bear on resolving some of the problems so rampant in the African-American community. You can rest assure that the pimp preacher is not moved with compassion to address any of these problems.

On the contrary, these are the very conditions which drive hopeless people to him looking for spiritual sustenance to help them cope in the face of their despair, in the first place. If a church purchases a grocery store, the economic effects would be immediate and profound. First of all, there would be an automatic customer base, the congregation. Secondly, there would be jobs for members of the same congregation. Thirdly and perhaps most importantly, the experience would create and promote entrepreneurial activity in the African-American community.

Furthermore, the success of such a venture would serve as a poignantly positive example of empowerment and self-determination for those who have long had the desire but have lacked the confidence to step out on this kind of powerful faith. It is past time that the African-American clergy realized that yes, the church must begin to take an active role in the economic development of the community. Those who are too self-indulgent, backwards, or hopelessly reactionary in their thinking, must be pulled kicking and screaming into this realization, or simply pushed aside, because the community can no longer afford to support these parasites. Preachers must find a way to combine their "milk and honey in heaven" message with the stark reality that the people must have the means to provide "bacon and eggs" right here on earth. The African-American church's dismal failure to adequately address the true spiritual and natural needs of the people will only result in the continuation of the maintenance of the sorry status quo. The church, for the most part, will remain irrelevant and impotent when it comes to dealing with the real bread and butter issues of the African-American community. Its power will remain only potential if its focus continues to be purely pseudo-spiritual. The need for self-empowerment and community development is too great because the withering poverty, massive unemployment, and utter hopelessness are too acute.

This is why most young African-American men spurn the church because, in their view, it really offers them nothing that they can see which could improve their daily lives. They can see no place for them in the church. So, consequently, they view its religious dogma about the, "Hereafter" as obsolete, irrelevant, and escapist. Therefore, the black church's message is

36

no different from, and certainly nowhere near as potent or profitable as the drugs that they can find in the streets. Therefore, there must be a new approach if the church is going to ever exercise even a fraction of its potential power to effectively deal with the myriad of problems vexing the African-American community. Those who truly know the way as God has given them the vision to see the way must rise up and push aside these pimp preachers along with all other servile perpetrators exploiting God's people for their own selfish and perverse gain.

CHAPTER 3

The Punk Preacher

The "Punk Preacher" is a personality type that is as pervasive in the African-American church as the pimp preacher. While the punk preacher personality type has some of the same latent traits as the pimp preacher, there are some more dominant and pronounced personality traits which make the two types different and clearly distinguishable. First of all, the punk preacher's style of leadership is strikingly similar to that of many black politicians. He or she merely sniffs the social winds of the congregation to ascertain the popular sentiment, and whatever it happens to be at any given time, that sentiment becomes the primary focus of the leadership. In other words, they lead from the rear and are never out front on any issue because they have a morbid fear of being out of step with the popular will. The punk preacher is far more concerned with being popular and politically correct, than being biblically sound and spiritually in tune with the God that, he professes to serve. As a result, the main focus of this kind of leadership is to make people feel emotionally good and intellectually comfortable with themselves, whether they choose to live a true Christian life or not. As long as they show up for worship service and keep the financial support coming, the punk preacher is more than satisfied.

The punk preacher is willing to tell the parishioners anything that will tickle their ears and make them feel comfortable with themselves. Consequently in these kinds of church congregations there is all manner of wickedness and corruption, as each member does as he or she pleases and becomes haughtily self-righteous in their own eyes. As a result, there is all kind of ungodly activity going on right in the church and the punk preacher is well aware of it. Moreover, he is usually a regular participant in this same rampant sin. Therefore the punk preacher's leadership is spiritually dysfunctional, morally gelded, and totally ineffective. Why? Because, he is a pitiful example of the very religion that he professes. Consequently, punk preachers preside over churches that are, for the most part, spiritually dead and morally bankrupt. Therefore, these kinds of churches stand as glaring examples of everything that a true church is certainly not supposed to be. This is why the black church has lost most of its historical respect and moral authority in the African-American community. So the punk preacher's primary concern is, to be, and remain popular, with his congregation by any means necessary. The punk preacher is first and foremost concerned with making the congregation feel good, complacent in its carnality, and comfortable enough with itself to continue its financial support, thus maintaining the clergy in its gaudy and ostentatious lifestyle. Therefore, these preachers are nothing more than whitewashed tombs with dead men bones. *Matthew 23:27*, "Woe unto you, scribes and Pharisees, hypocrites! For ye are like unto whited sepulchers which indeed appear beautiful outward, but are within full of dead men bones, and are all unclean." Verse 28: "Even so ye also outwardly appear righteous unto men, but within ye are full of hypocrisy and iniquity."

Punk preachers preside over churches that have a form of Godliness, but they deny the power thereof. *II Tim. 3: 5.* They are hopelessly blind to the true shamefulness of their own hypocrisy and they have become brazen and even narcissistic in their own arrogance as they go about their business of practicing what they call, Christianity. These punk preachers have absolutely no spiritual walk, redemptive example, or moral influence, even within their own congregations. As a result, they stand as the worst examples of religious hypocrisy in the African-American community. In his obsessive determination to be popular and persuasive with the flock in order to maintain the financial support, the punk preacher becomes only a sham as a spiritual leader and a hopeless hypocrite as a Christian example. Consequently, this makes for the jaded practice of Christianity according to him a tragic exercise in self-delusion.

The second glaring trait of the punk preacher is his skill at managing conflict. This could, and should be an admirable quality in any leader. However, the punk preacher has managed to turn it into something negative and perverse. In their frantic determination to keep the illusion of peace at all cost, punk preachers will plot, plan, and scheme in order to subvert the best interest of their own congregations. For example, how many times have you witnessed this kind of scenario? Joe blow has been a long time member of the church. He pays his tithes and gives handsomely in the collection plate every week. However, it has been rumored that Joe Blow has been fooling around with Deacon Jones' wife. Now Joe Blow is married, but because of his bad temper and large imposing figure,

40

it is believed that his little timid wife is afraid of him. So she remains silent and seemingly oblivious to the talk that has been circulating concerning her husband and deacon Jones' wife.

Deacon Jones is an older man in poor health and may know, or at least have some suspicion of what is going on. He has not confronted Joe Blow directly but has brought this matter to the pastor. The pastor, rather than confront Joe Blow or the wife of the deacon in question, elects to overlook the entire matter since he said no one has actually seen them doing anything. Now whether the allegations against Joe Blow and the deacon's wife were true or not, the preacher has the moral responsibility as the pastor of the congregation to at least bring the matter to the attention of the parties involved. The very scriptures that he is supposed to be guided by demand as much. "We should flee from the very appearance of sin." *I These. 5:23.* However, to keep peace and perhaps more importantly to keep Joe Blow's financial support, the punk preacher decided that no action was the best action.

Here is another scenario. There is an unruly member of the young adult choir, who has been causing tremendous problems for the entire group. This particular young woman has a beautiful voice, and the ability to move people with the passion of her singing. However, she has no respect for the choir director's ability to lead the choir. Consequently, she argues over every aspect of the choir practice. There are other choir members who are fed up with her. The choir director, herself, realizes that the presence of this unruly individual has severely damaged the morale of the entire group. Therefore she, the director has taken the matter before the pastor.

The punk preacher who is already aware of the situation and had been contented to let matters continue perhaps as long as he possibly could was now forced to address the situation. The first thing that he proceeded to do was to balance this woman's apparent talent and her popularity with the rest of the congregation, against the trouble that she was causing in the choir. He decided needless to say, not to confront the trouble-maker and shifted the whole matter totally back on the shoulders of the weary choir director. So he advised them to pray for her and bear with her. The Lord would work things out. This is one of the classic ploys that the punk preacher uses to escape his responsibility as a mediator of conflict as spiritual leader in the church. "Yes, I know that there is a problem, but let's let the Lord work it out." "He said that He's going to let the wheat and the tares grow together and He will do the separating." *Matthew 13:24-30*, in actuality, this approach absorbs the punk preacher of any real responsibility to discipline and correct members of the congregation whose unchristian behavior tends to have a very damaging effect on other members.

There is yet another scenario among many that I have personally witnessed. There was an individual who was in charge of running the sound equipment that was used during the praise and worship service in a church that I once attended. This particular individual had a very abrupt way of talking to people. Many times his manner seemed down right abrasive, especially when someone dared to question him or attempted to give any input regarding the operation of the sound system. Eventually the problem with this individual's behavior got back to the preacher, whom I am certain, already knew about it and simply lacked the spiritual backbone to deal with him. Because of the preacher's refusal to even bring the matter to the individual's attention, we were forced to endure his behavior that was the source of great anxiety and tension among many members. Eventually, the situation escalated to the point where it exploded in a vicious argument. Feelings were needlessly hurt and tension lingered long after because the punk preacher did not have the natural backbone and the spiritual conviction required of his position as pastor, to deal forth rightly and effectively with the matter when it first came to his attention. These are just several examples of the wholesale inter personal strife, rivalries, and other forms of debilitating conflict between the various cliques, clans, and factions which seethe and boil just below the placid surface of religious tranquility, in many a congregation shepherded by these punk preachers. They are so obsessed with managing conflict and displaying a demeanor of Christianity, that their dubious efforts are purely an exercise in style and form rather than spiritual substance. This total abandonment of spiritual principles, and moral conviction makes the punk preacher one of the main culprits in the spiritual impotency and moral decay of the black church.

The punk preacher stands as a tragic mockery and pathetic contradiction to everything that the true Christian life style represents. Ironically, he is the exact opposite of everything out lined in the very

Bible in which he claims to adhere. The punk preacher represents that church which has long lost its savor as the salt of the earth and is therefore no good for anything, except to be trampled under the feet of men, *Matt. 5:13*. Finally I will discuss the punk preacher's total abdication of any responsibility for the spiritual growth and moral development of the church body. There is virtually no commitment to the teaching of those very spiritual principles and precepts in which they profess to the world to believe and embrace. This scandalous lack of commitment to the teaching and practice of religious doctrine has merely perpetuated and legitimized the pervasive hypocrisy; thus giving rise to the current disastrously debilitating state of affairs in these churches. Paradoxically, these assemblies are churches in name and edifice only. For behind those consecrated walls all manner of shenanigan and perverse human intrigue are practiced. Consequently, "Where there is no vision, the people perish". As the scripture says in *II Chronicles 7:14*, "If my people, which are called by my name, shall humble themselves, and pray, and seek my face and turn from their wicket ways, then will I hear from heaven, and will forgive their sin, and will heel their land."

The punk preacher's pseudo-commitment to the true gospel is nothing more than a stylized game of the most insidious form of deception. In his real commitment to minimize and control conflict in the congregation and maintain the appearance of Holy harmony, the religious practice has become that of pretension and self-delusion. By assuming no real commitment to the gospel, therefore, there is no responsibility for actually preaching and teaching it. As a result, the gospel in these churches represents nothing more than the Bibles owned by the members, and the hymnals in back of the pews. In other words, Christianity has become nothing more than a cheap label, and church, only a generic term to refer to the kind of scandalous activity which is anything but Christian.

Punk preachers understand that the absence of true commitment to their professed principles and beliefs does not obligate them to be committed to anything else. As a result, many critical and crucial issues affecting the very lives of the church faithful are not addressed. Therefore, critical issues like teen pregnancy, drug addiction, crime, joblessness, hopelessness, and family disintegration are too controversial for punk preachers. This is because they may have to confront and correct members who are on the wrong side of these issues. As a result, any and all conceivable nonsense and unbridled wickedness is tolerated. In other words, anything goes. "We are not to judge," I've often heard preachers say, "that is God's business." Matthew 7:1-5 says, "Judge not, that ye be not judged." Well then, what exactly are we to do, simply continue to turn our collective heads and merely close our eyes to the spiritual debauchery now so pervasive and running rampant in the church? This notion of non-confrontation of sin and unchristian behavior has only served to make the perpetrators of such sin, feel justified, and even self-righteous in their own wickedness. So, punk preachers feel no compunction to tell the congregation what, thus saith the Lord. Their unmitigated refusal to embrace and commit to the gospel gives them no standard.

Therefore, where there is no standard, there is no standard to uphold. There is no one standing in the gap, challenging so-called Christians to live up to those spiritual principles and precepts, that they've so piously professed to the world, that they have committed their lives to. There is no necessity to teach people how to apply the word of God to their daily lives in order that they may grow in their understanding of God and be better disciples of Jesus Christ. The very absence of these punk preacher's own commitment to the Christian doctrine that they profess, is compelling evidence that they are spiritually disqualified to serve as a creditable example of a true Christian to their church flocks or the community at large. Therefore, their lofty platitudes about what God can do, and how good he is, are as hollow as echoes in the wind. The members of the congregations are not fooled. They know, who and what, their pastors are.

So again the potential power of the church is squandered on hypocrisy and petty self-indulgence by punk preachers, who are, nothing more than wolves dressed in sheep's clothing. *Matthew 7:15,* these rascals have been ready and more than willing to bastardize the scriptures and beguile the faithful. As a result, the church's legitimate moral authority to sanction sinful behavior, which has been the major obstacle to the spiritual growth and maturity of the entire black church body, has been, and continues to be, all but non-existent. The church's primary strength has been historically its moral influence over its members and non-members alike. The very legitimacy of its moral authority has been predicated on the community's belief in the churches spiritual

46

validity and its moral conviction. In other words, the church was in fact, practicing that which it purported to stand for. Over the years however, the church's once Spartan reputation has grown progressively tarnished. The brazenly excessive and scandalous indulgences on the part of the black clergy, over the years, have done much to render the moral influence of the church on the community all but totally ineffective. This is why these punk preachers must go. They are an abomination to God and a scourge on the once respectable image of the black church.

Whose responsibility is it to get rid of these self-indulgent leeches? It is the responsibility of those good and decent souls who are honestly seeking to be Disciples of Christ. The example of Jesus Christ should and ought to be the criteria or standard by which church leaders and congregation alike are to be measured. It is clearly out lined in parables and other scriptures through out the Bible, the spiritual well being of an individual, or lack there of. The tree is known by the fruit that it bears, Matthew 6:16-20. There is fruit of the spirit and there is the works of the flesh and the bible clearly delineates the differences between each, and then spells out the consequences of each kind of fruit. *Gal. 5:19-21.* Delineates the works of the flesh and *Gal. 5:22-23*, delineates the fruit of the Spirit.

Therefore, good and decent people honestly trying to follow Christ must not allow these punk preachers to manipulate the bible and pervert its spiritual intent in order to support their carnal lifestyles and wicked and selfish machinations. True Christians are commanded: to love that which God loves and hate that which he hates. Yes, the bible also requires that Christians be forgiving, but this notion of forgiveness should not, and in fact, does not mean that Christians are obliged to except and accommodate the pathetic and brazing wickedness currently running so rampant and unchallenged in the church. The tolerance and close- mouthed posture of many church congregations to this kind of scandalous behavior, appears to the unbelieving, that it is tacitly approved of. If the church is ever going to fulfill its mission on earth as God intended, those who are sincere in their own commitment to follow Christ, have to stand up for what they say that they believe. In an age where society seems to be suffering from an acute condition of moral and spiritual decay, the church is the last bulwark against the total collapse of spirituality and morality.

If the spiritual decay and moral decadence of the general society is allowed to penetrate, permeate, and pollute the sanctity of the church, then the church will have lost its very power to redeem fallen humanity. In an age where people seem to be completely amoral, where everything and anything goes, the church must be, first and foremost, a spiritual and moral example for it's faithful, and the larger black community. Then, it must also rise up and assume its role as an agent for spiritual and moral uplift and economic empowerment for the African-American community. The black church must be that beacon, that spiritual lighthouse that can guide black folk, who seemed to be predisposed to self-destruction and destroying one another, to a higher plain of human relations.

The church must once and for all, confront the black man's worst malady, the internalized belief in his own innate inferiority. He has inevitably embraced these deep-seated feelings of self-hatred which has been a consequence of centuries of systematic indoctrination with the myth of black inferiority. Therefore, he has been taught to have an unmitigated hatred for himself and everything black or African. Furthermore, he has been totally written out of the scriptures in the European version of the bible. He has been left thoroughly ignorant of the fact that the only authentic version of the Holy Bible is actually his own story. Yet, the African has been recast and redefined by racists white European Biblical writers, as sub-human, and a primitive being without a soul, worthless, and insignificant in human civilization. This is the monumental task that awaits the true Christian church. It must restore, reclaim, and rejuvenate a people who are not only lost and estranged from God, but also lost and estranged from themselves. Therefore, only a spiritually legitimate and morally sound church, qualified and equipped by the living God of the universe, can provide black men and women with the proper spiritual and moral frame of reference for relating to each other and living Holy and righteous lives on this earth. In light of the grinding poverty, escalating crime, and utter hopelessness so pervasive and profound in the African-American community, the church must rise up and play a more positive and pivotal role in the affairs of that community. It is said that the African-American church is the actual heart and soul of the community. If this is the case, then it is high time that it rose up and assumed its rightful role. The time is too far spent to wait for the federal, state, or local governments to solve the debilitating problems affecting the African-American community. It should be painfully apparent that after decades of shameful neglect, that this is not going to happen.

Therefore, those institutions and organizations within the community have to step forward and take on more responsibility for the very survival of their own community. Any leader, church or otherwise, who does not recognize the dire straits of the inner city African-American community and is not moved with compassion to address these problems, doesn't really stand for anything, and therefore, should be dismissed for the nothing that he or she is. Any church that does not challenge men and women to live up to the Christian principles and convictions they say to the world, that they embrace, is not worth your support. Furthermore, it is not even worth your time and attention. Why, because, it is definitely not going to enhance you spiritually, morally, or otherwise. Therefore those who seek the truth, must watch as well as pray, Ephesians 6:18. "How can the blind lead the blind, less they both fall into a ditch"? *Matthew 15:12-14.*

It will be up to those decent and sincere souls who are diligently seeking God who will lead them into all righteousness, and who will ultimately be the ones God will equip and qualify to lead His people out of the darkness of generations of ignorance into the bright sunshine of His divine wisdom. A sincere and faithful Christian is the punk preacher's greatest nemesis. Why, because fidelity will always stand as a stark contrast and poignant example in the face of infidelity. Veracity will always expose hypocrisy. A committed and obedient Christian life will always expose the uncommitted and disobedient, carnal life. Finally, faithfulness will always expose faithlessness, especially, when they are in such close proximity as the same church congregation. So, faithfulness, obedience, commitment, compassion, sincerity, honesty, conviction, forgiveness, and true Christian love, all of these things are the very antithesis of what punk preachers represent. Therefore, they stand out as glaring examples of who they really are: wolves in sheep clothing. Consequently these wolves in sheep clothing are only there to deceive, beguile, and exploit those honest souls who are sincerely seeking a relationship with God and trying to do His will. This is what really makes punk preachers such despicable characters. They have no compunction in their shameful effort to pervert and exploit this genuine sincerity of decent folk. These punk preachers not only have no commitment to the true gospel, they also are without any legitimate morals, ethics, or principles. They are guided only by their own lust, greed, and petty self-indulgence, which is the gospel according to them. These empty-hearted and greedy-minded characters only see the church as an organization ripe for exploitation, not as an organism to be spiritually cultivated and developed in the image of Christ. This is why these punk preachers must go, the church can no longer afford to be bled dry by these insatiable parasites. Their presence represents not only a financial drain on the church's resources, but they stand as the major obstruction to the spiritual development and moral maturity of the church. The church will never be all that God intended it to be, unless or until, it is purged of these parasites who have robbed it of its spiritual vitality and moral legitimacy.

Again, honest and decent people who are sincerely seeking to do the will of God must truly amerce themselves in His word and pray for His divine guidance. They must stop looking exclusively to these phony, rip-off artists masquerading as preachers and look to God for their spiritual guidance. Follow the preacher only if he is following Christ, *1st Cor. 11:1.* How will you know if your preacher is truly following Christ? You will know only if you are following Christ. When you truly belong to Him, really sold out to Christ and committed your life to Him he will not allow you to be tricked or fooled by anyone. When you truly belong to Him, you will know it, because you will have his spirit living inside of you. This is called the Holy Ghost. He will lead and guide you into all righteousness, and be your teacher, instructing you in the perfect will of Christ. *John,14:26.* This does not mean that you do not have to read and study the bible. On the contrary, you must study as the scripture commands, in order to show yourself approved unto God, *II Timothy, 2:15.* You must study because the primary way that the Holy Ghost will instruct you is through your study of the scriptures. As you begin to grow in grace and wisdom, you will be able to spot these punk preachers and moreover, have the spiritual boldness to confront them about their grievous sin.

Finally, again it will be the responsibility of the true Christians to clean up the church and make it what it could, and should be. Those who think that they are enlightened and informed, but who set back in their smug piety looking down their sanctimonious noses at the church being ripped off and exploited by these charlatans, are in fact, just as guilty. *Revelation 3:17-18*. Th, who knew his Lord's will and prepared not himself, shall be beaten with many strikes. *Luke 12:47-48*. The church is not in the sad state that it is, because of those who use it for all manner of wickedness and exploitation, but because those who know better and just sit back and elect to do absolutely nothing. The bible says that Christians are soldiers and that we are in a spiritual war with the devil. Therefore it is required and commanded of all Christians to put on the whole armor and stand up and fight against sin wherever it might exist and whomever is the perpetrator. *Ephesians 6:14-18*, How can any one lead God's people unless he or she be called of God? The only way to truly know this is to have God within you. Then you can try the spirit by the spirit living in you. Otherwise it is an exercise in utter futility to wait for the spiritually dead, morally bankrupt, and an insatiably exploitative clergy to attack the corruption and vice of which they are a part. As a result, churches are inundated with all manner of wickedness which looms in the eyes of the unbelievers as the very epitome of hypocrisy and pathetic examples of shameful self-delusion.

In a world where there seems to be no standard for judging right and wrong, good and evil, morality and immorality, the church instead of being a spiritual lighthouse and standard bearer of God's rules of right-eous behavior, has all but succumbed to the mass insanity around it. The tremendous incidence of teenage pregnancy, single parent households, alco-holism, and drug abuse, high school drop out, job-lessness, and violence have virtually devastated the inner city; these very critical issues vexing the African-American community must be dealt with by the church. It must raise men and women in the fear and admonition of God. Only these men and women will have the spiritual enlightenment and intestinal fortitude to shepherd God's flock. We must have the kind of Christian warriors who will move in the power of God. Holy ghost filled, sanctified, leaders who will have the back bone to stand up against the forces of sin, wickedness, and corruption which have enslaved the minds of so many of our people and have locked them in a state of perpetual poverty and utter hopelessness. Yes, the black church with correct spiritual teaching, moral legitimacy, and its enormous financial strength could, and should indeed, play a pivotal role in reversing the ravages of sin which have all but destroyed the inner-cities and have reeked almost irreparable damage upon the African-American community as a whole.

CHAPTER 4

The Pusher Preacher

The "Pusher Preacher" is another personality type that is just as pervasive in the African-American church as the pimp and the punk preachers. As a result, the effect of the pusher preacher's presence is just as destructive. The most pronounced traits of the pusher preacher are delineated here. First of all, he has an incredible capacity to sell the notion of the after life as being the fundamental idea, and exclusive focus of Christianity. Secondly, he has an uncanny ability to wrap himself in religious mysticism in order to appear legitimately prophetic. Thirdly, he is woefully lacking in his ability to translate the theoretical precepts of Christian dogma into practical application with regard to daily living. The pusher preacher just like his counterpart on the streets, boulevards, and avenues that crisscross the urban centers of America has become a permanent fixture as a dream merchant in the church.

The pusher preacher has created and promoted a myth that is as powerful as any narcotic which declares, in essence, that all you have to do is endure and suffer for his namesake. You need to accept your plight, no matter how economically wretched, socially debilitating, or psychologically crippling it may be. Just accept your miserable lot here on this earth with gladness, because God will reward your suffering with a starry crown in heaven. This spiritually intoxicating and emotionally retarding concoction of half-truths is the tremendously potent hallucinogen that is the stock and trade of the pusher preacher. Congregations force-fed on a steady diet of this psychologically crippling, socially withering, and emotionally traumatizing dogma in the name of Christianity, become the pliant, docile, and pathetically quiescent citizens who are the poor souls conditioned by their religion, to live in communities inundated with abject poverty, rampant violence, and total governmental neglect. This is why it is far less difficult to get such people out to sing, dance, and pray at a church meeting than it is to get them together to create a block watch program or other civic endeavors which would make life easier and their streets perhaps a bit safer.

The pusher preacher is not in the least concerned with the social or economic needs of his or her own congregation, nor those needs of the larger community. Instead he is obsessed with and totally focused on "the pie in the sky" notion of religion. The millions of honest and decent people, who have bought into this absurdly faulty notion of Christianity, have unwittingly bought into the grand delusion sold by these religious pushers. This is the most heinous fraud ever perpetrated against a people who have already been the greatest victims of social, psychological, and economic oppression in the history of the world. Of course, it is the true will of Jesus Christ that the believers inherit the Kingdom of Heaven, and have eternal life. However, it is also as much God's divine will for the believers to have an abundant life right

56

here and right now, on this earth. *III John Verse 2* This is the glaring omission in the pusher preacher's message. The reason why the notion of the abundant life, here on earth, is consciously and carefully omitted, is because the pusher preacher realizes that, a total focus on the here after never obligates him or her to take any risks or confront any real and immediate problems affecting the community. They are more than content to push those ideas like, "keep the faith"... "Hold on just a little while longer"... and "By and by when the morning comes, everything will be all right." Pusher preachers use these time-tested flim-flams on their congregations with sickening repetition, which are nothing more than hollow ideas suggesting the notion of ultimate triumph. I submit that it is just as reprehensible for the pusher preacher to perpetrate this hallucinogenic myth wrapped in religious dogma on the most helpless and hopeless segment of the African-American community as it is for the common drug dealer to push his or her wares on the same group. I also pray that this examination and correlation of this striking comparison between the street pusher and the pulpit pusher, will illicit the same kind of moral outrage and righteous indignation as good and decent people have had for the street dealer. I further submit that the pusher preacher, just as the drug dealer, only offers an unsuccessful attempt at escaping reality. As a result, the real cost of this exercise in escapism amid the continuing physical and moral deterioration of the community has been just as incalculably destructive in terms of the cost in mental health and loss in human potential as the consumption of illicit drugs.

People are being taught that it is God's divine will to live in grinding poverty, amid rampant crime, and among urban and rural blight. This kind of pseudo-religious shamming is beneath my contempt and the absolute epitome of religious exploitation. There is nothing Godly about having to live amid uncontrolled crime and vice. There is nothing at all holy about living in substandard housing or having access to inadequate medical care. There is nothing at all spiritual or spiritually redeeming about living among urban and rural decay, inadequate education and soaring unemployment. The pusher preacher's interpretation of the "pie in the sky" view of Christianity juxtaposed against the stark reality of living in inner city America is null and void. It is as empty as the hearts of the men and women pushing it. Nevertheless, it is as potent as the illicit narcotics pushed in the African-American community by the legions of greedy-minded, empty-hearted drug dealers. Consequently, it is spiritually, psychologically, and physically lethal in its emotionally intoxicating effect.

The next clearly recognizable trait of the pusher preacher is the seemingly compulsive need to wrap himself in religious mysticism. They have convinced themselves that they are the true shepherds of God and they are the only ones who really know the mind of God and his divine will for the flock. Many of them set about displaying strange or eccentric manners ostensibly to impress people with their mysticism and convince them of their authenticity. They are willing to go to any level of absurdity in order to convince people that they are indeed the only truly ordained Shepherds of God's flock. Some of these pusher preachers, as I have stated, will affect many odd or weird behaviors in an attempt to set themselves apart from the rest of the members of their congregations. These behaviors may range from a significantly different style of dress, speech, and sleeping or eating habits, thus affecting the appearance of extreme social aloofness or a life totally unconcerned with the practical matters of everyday living. Many of them will claim to have a very close relationship with God. These claims will range from having super natural abilities to heel the sick, to actually knowing the very thoughts of God Himself, to having the ability to understand all mysteries of the Bible and being able to interpret all spiritual gifts as well as discerning them in others. All these things are quite rampant in those churches pastored by pusher preachers. The pusher preachers are so holy that they are actually obsolete in their very function as pastors. Why? Because they themselves are so disconnected from the daily living experience of their own flock that they cannot possibly serve as an example of practical Christian living.

Many decent people, who are searching for the God of their salvation and looking for the evidence of His spirit, are taken in by these charlatans. They are impressed by the illusion of genuine holiness affected by these pusher preachers, and by their stylized eccentricities, which have been perfected through years of practiced deception. The acid test is the message. Is the message that this individual brings, the true and unadulterated gospel of Jesus Christ? Is he really preaching the death, burial, resurrection of Christ, and the redemptive power of his love and grace? Is he actually preaching about God's divine will, that people can only be His disciples by being living examples of what Jesus Christ represents? Is the preacher a living example of what he professes? The Bible clearly places a believing heart and committed life at the top of the list of the spiritual imperatives that one must satisfy in order to be a true disciple of Jesus Christ. It guarantees that an individual's fruit will ultimately reveal to the world whether or not there is in fact any relationship with God. No amount of spiritual perpetration or stylized posturing can compensate for a true believing heart and committed life to that which one professes to believe as spiritual truth. Therefore, the true believer can only be known by the fruit that he or she bears.

In these churches, the premium placed on the incidence and exercising of spiritual gifts has gone from the sublime to the absurd. There has been far too much attention focused on speaking in tongues, the interpretation of tongues, prophesying, and preaching. Yet, there has been nowhere near enough time and attention devoted to actually teaching folk how to live right before God and how to be true Christian examples before non-believers. The preoccupation with religious mysticism has become the means to an end for the pusher preacher and has, as a result, shamefully denigrated the real effect of spiritual gifts and their rightful place in the church. To pusher preachers, it is far more important to wrap themselves in a cloak of religious mysticism in a vain attempt at validation and legitimize their supposed spiritual authority, than to represent any credible example of the true Christian lifestyle.

Consequently, they engage in the frantic pursuit of this mystical persona or spiritual guru, whom they seem convinced, will yield spiritual legitimacy. In fact, the pushers only serve to alienate themselves from the very flock that they purport to serve. In other words, it only makes them that much more obsolete and ineffectual as legitimate spiritual leaders. Finally, the pusher preacher seems to be totally unaware or just patently unconcerned that this headlong flight into religious mysticism simply creates a gulf between preacher and congregation, which makes the application of the true spiritual precepts of Christianity to practical daily living impossible. Why? Because the leader has donned such a mystical persona that makes him appear so different, the average parishioner cannot grasp the practical application of his message or the earthly significance of his life. Therefore, the pusher preacher's lofty claims of his great knowledge, wisdom, and prophecy only looms as empty bombast especially, when the average parishioner tries to reconcile them with the reality of the sorry condition of the church's faithful. If these pusher preachers have all these divine gifts and all this super natural power, then why aren't they using it to improve the spiritual, social, and economic condition of the flock? So it is this glaring discrepancy between the spiritual and the natural that makes the message of these pusher preachers, for all its boast and bombast, hollow, ineffective, and obsolete in the face of the moral, social, and economic decay of the African-American community.

The third most pronounced trait of the pusher preacher is his pathetic inability or blatant disinterest in teaching or translating the spiritual precepts of Christianity into practical lessons for daily living. This, without a doubt, is the single most dismal failure of the African-American clergy as a whole. However, it is one of the most poignantly glaring omissions of the pusher preacher's message. The pusher preacher's almost single-minded focus on the promotion of the "pie in the sky" notion of Christianity, along with the preoccupation with effecting, and perfecting the persona of religious mystic, have left virtually no time or attention to teaching the practical application of Christianity. This abysmal disparity of focus and discrepancy between precept and practice is one of the greatest ironies and rankest form of hypocrisy in the African-American Church as a whole. I submit that it is the cruelest form of mockery to tell a believer that his or her father owns the cattle on a thousand hills and they don't have, and do not know where to get, the money to buy a jug of milk or a single steak. *Psalms 5:10*. It is immoral, unethical, and downright criminal to tell people that, "The earth is the Lord's and the fullness thereof and he will supply all of your needs according to his riches in glory." *Psalms 50:10*, without teaching them how to establish and develop an intimate relationship with this God. *Philippians 4:1*. It is utter futility to tell people that they are a part of a royal priesthood, and sons and daughters of the living God, without teaching them who God really is, and showing them how to internalize these precepts and truly take them to heart.

Those spiritual principles and precepts outlined in the Christian Bible combine to form one of the best blueprints for human existence on this planet.

However, the problem is with the interpretation and application of the Bible. This fact is nowhere more apparent than among those churches led by these pusher preachers. Jesus Christ often used parables to teach the people spiritual principles and precepts. He used these earthly stories to reveal heavenly principles. He knew that by using stories about things that the people were familiar with and could relate to, he could reach and teach them. He talked about farming, sheep herding, housekeeping, banquets and other things that were part of their culture and daily lives. He was able to teach the people, through his word and by example, about his Father. He not only told people how to live, but He showed them by His example how to live. He challenged them and encouraged them that they would by their faith and obedience do greater things than He did. John 14: 12-14: Jesus Christ set the standard for church leadership with His method of preaching and teaching, as well as the criteria for discipleship by His living example. The apostle John called Jesus Christ the living word. John 1: 14. "And the word was made flesh and dwelt among us, and we beheld his glory, the glory as of the only begotten of the Father, full of grace and truth." Then Jesus Christ showed the world by his living example, how to be faithful and true to that which one professes. He also promised, that if we abide in Him, He would abide in us, and in Him we can truly overcome any suffering, sin, or evil in the world. John 15:5-7: This is the rich and powerful part of Christ's message to the believers that pusher preachers have so sorely neglected to bring to the faithful.

Oh yes, it is God's will that the believers shall inherit the Kingdom of Heaven, but it is also His will that those same believers shall also have healthy and prosperous lives right here, and right now, on this earth. John 10:9-10: This is where pusher preachers, along with the vast majority of the African-American clergy in general, are tragically lacking in their ability to interpret and teach the total will of God. I submit that they are just too morally bankrupt, spiritually dysfunctional, and intellectually limited to lead God's people. These pusher preachers are not only out of place, but they are out of touch and out of step with the people that they purport to lead.

With the flood tide of drugs and crime coupled with the debilitating physical decay of the inner city where many African-Americans have to call home, the church must rise up and play a more substantial role in combating these problems. It must be forced to come to grips with the guilelessness of its gelded message, with the shameful hollowness of its pomposity, and the utter absurdity of its bombastic claims of power when it remains virtually impotent. It must be forced to reconcile theory with practice, standing with state, and walk with talk. It is an exercise of utter futility to continue to spout religious dogma that is impotent, obsolete, and totally irrelevant to the daily lives of the people. The church must reconcile these discrepancies or it will merely continue to contribute to, and further compound the chronic problems affecting African Americans. The black church can no longer hide its pious head in the sand like the proverbial ostrich, and mouth sanctimonious platitudes, while the community around it sinks deeper into the spiritual, social, and economic abyss.

It will be the cruelest self-delusion to stand back and wait for these pimp, punk, and pusher preachers to step forward and do the right thing. This will never happen. The chronic problems so entrenched, and so pervasive in the African-American community can only be honestly and forthrightly addressed when decent men and women stand up and demand that their leaders address the real problems of the congregation and community at large. The true believers must be more watchful and prayerful and a great deal more circumspect in the kind of people that they allow to stand behind the sacred desk calling themselves preachers. Many are called, but few are chosen and still fewer are sent to do the real work of God. Matthew 22:1-14: There are too many self- appointed preachers and family-run churches. This is one of the contributing factors of the success and proliferation of the kind of people who shouldn't be allowed anywhere nears a pulpit. However, once these individuals manage to gain control in a given church, they never rest until their control is absolute. Even if the church has a deacon board, or group of elders, these individuals are able to gain control and have their way through ingratiation, manipulation, and various other insidious means of human intrigue. The pimp, punk and pusher preachers are all very adept and consummately skilled at the manipulation and exploitation of people. Finally, the pusher preacher is not in the least concerned with the glaring discrepancy between the spiritual standing and the natural state of the average parishioner, because again, this is simply not his function. Furthermore, the pusher preacher has no compunction about trying to reconcile these paradoxes. Therefore, he sees no discrepancy, no irony, and no paradox. For he is spiritually dead, morally bankrupt, and a deathless, blood-sucking leech fastened to the jugular vein of the black church.

CHAPTER 5

The African-American Church as an Educational Institution

The African-American church has a tremendous potential as an educational institution. Unfortunately, this prospect has never really been exploited anywhere near its fullest potential. In the early days of this republic, the church was the primary agent for educating children. Churches were the forerunners of the schoolhouses. For decades after the formation of this nation as an independent republic, churches were the primary vehicles for the education of white children. Even after the advent of public schools, and the idea of universal education took root in America for white children, the church continued to play an important role in education. During, and directly after the civil war when the notion of education of the former slaves gained some measure of popular acceptance and support in the north, it was primarily the white church denominations that were in the forefront of this movement.

Many of these denominations had also been in the forefront of the abolitionist movement and the necessity to educate the ex-slave was the logical progression of their efforts. Therefore, thousands of white men and women went south to teach and train those newly liberated slaves how to survive in their newly found freedom. Consequently, most of the efforts in educating the former slaves were put forth by white church denominations. Subsequently, African-American counterparts of these basically white Protestant denominations began to spring up through out the former confederacy and the black church assumed a pivotal role in the education of the ex-slaves. Most of the schools of higher education established for the education of the ex-slave during reconstruction and thereafter, were established by white Protestant denominations. Many of them such as Hampton Institute, Fisk, Tuskegee, Wilberforce, Overland College, Lincoln, and Shaw University have survived until this day. These and many other historically black colleges, born as a result of the largess of white

Protestant church denominations still are about the business of educating African-Americans. Similarly, those Negro protestant denominations which were established and evolved after the close of the civil war also played an integral role in the establishment and maintenance of African-American academic and vocational schools. Since the days of reconstruction and the subsequent restoration of home rule in the south, with the removal of the federal troops that had been placed there to protect the civil rights of the newly freed slaves, the church has been instrumental in the education of the freedmen. However, with the restoration of home rule in the south with the Hayes-Tillman compromise of 1877, the former white power structure reasserted itself throughout the south. Immediately, this resurrected white power elite implemented a system of black codes that totally disenfranchised southern blacks by 1890. The Hayes-Tillman Compromise allowed these former confederates to finally wrest control of their state governments from federal domination after a feeble attempt at Northern sponsored Reconstruction. Then these unrepentant rebels set about to reduce the black man to his former slave status by severely limiting his political, social, and economic life. As a result, the church, in most cases, was the only vehicle available for educating the former slaves.

The Jim Crow schools for blacks, what few there were, throughout the south were woefully inadequate and pathetically under-funded. The very political leaders who had run the former confederacy administered them. The racial and economic caste system created for blacks during the birth of this nation was primarily controlled by the white landed aristocracy. However, the very physical foundation of this nation was built and maintained by the free labor of millions of African slaves. Moreover, it was maintained for decades after the end of legal slavery by the children of twenty generations of African slaves. Most white historians have gone to absurd extremes in their vain attempts to portray the American South during the early days of this nation as a romanticized agrarian culture of chivalrous gentlemen and grand ladies. They have endeavored to create all manner of idealized myths while carefully leaving out the brutal facts of American life during this vaunted period. These white historians have skillfully skirted the facts which testify to the bottomless barbarity and sadistic savagery systematically perpetrated against blacks in a philosophy of the economic development of this continent which had African slavery as its very cornerstone. However, when the nation became polarized and eventually split into two sections over a difference of opinion among the white power elite as to what approach America would take concerning the economic and political use of the black man as it entered into the Industrial Revolution, there was a civil war. The North, because of its superior economic might and abundance of available manpower, finally defeated the South after a long bloody war. The American Civil War destroyed slavery and left most of the South lying in smoldering ruins. Nevertheless, these vanquished but brazenly unregenerate rebels were not about to see the freedmen elevated to a level of political, economic and social equality with them. Consequently, they made certain that the kinds of economic and political opportunities that would afford such equality to the Negro would not be available to him through a combination of legislation, isolation, intimidation, and terrorism. Therefore, the church was the only viable alternative for the education of the Negro. Consequently church-run and church-supported schools marshaled their meager resources and shouldered the burden admirably. Hence the African-American church has been there from the beginning and has put forth a stupendous effort in the education of the Negro.

The urbanization and industrialization of America after the turn of the century caused many southern legislatures to be swept along by the winds of economic change. For, in the face of social and political pressure from northern white industrialists doing business in the south, they had to grudgingly upgrade their efforts to educate the Negro population. Furthermore, the beginning of World War II brought the mass migration of Negroes from the south to take advantage of the jobs that were created by the critical demand for laborers in wartime industries. With the assumption of the higher living wages that these jobs afforded, the Negro population north and south began to agitate for the same citizenship rights as white Americans.

This political pressure translated into the gradual removal of some of the social and economic barriers that had been erected to preclude the full participation of blacks in American life. One of these areas was the integration of many of the state institutions of higher education. Shortly thereafter came the Brown decision which decreed the abolition of the infamous separate but equal doctrine instituted by the *Plessy vs. Ferguson* Supreme court decision in 1896. This Plessy versus Ferguson Supreme Court decision had set forth a legal doctrine of "Separate but Equal." This meant that there was to be a total and complete physical separation of black and white people in all matters of public accommodations. As a result, America became a dual society sanctioned and buttressed by the force of law. She was already a dual society which had been sanctioned by her racist customs, and traditions that had all but totally separated black and white Americans, socially, since the inception of the nation. However, with the, *Plessy vs Ferguson* decision in 1896, the United States Supreme Court legitimized and crystallized the force of these social customs and traditions into Federal Law.

This was in effect the legal apartheid that locked African Americans into a racial caste system that totally barred them from any meaningful participation in the social, economic, and political life of this nation for more than sixty years. African Americans, as a group, have never recovered from this damnable and insidious government sanctioned oppression. The effects are still painfully apparent and even the most naive mind cannot deny that African Americans have been irreparably damaged by America's racial caste system of legal apartheid. While the judiciary and executive branches of government were extremely meticulous in seeing to it that black and white people were kept separate in their public accommodations, they were not nearly so meticulous in making sure that those accommodations were equal. On the contrary, they made sure that those public accommodations, especially in the area of public education for blacks remain inferior to that afforded whites. This was to insure that "Niggers" would always remain in their proper place that of an inherently inferior social, political, and economic position in relation to whites.

Finally, in 1954, the Warren court was eventually shamed into overturning that legal apartheid, in the Brown decision. However, neither the United States Supreme Court nor any other branch of government has done anything significant in the intervening years, to remedy the tremendous damage done by "Separate but Equal". During this time after the Brown decision, while the federal government was making its half-hearted effort to put pressure on the states north and south to improve black education, the church seemed to lessen its role, especially in primary and secondary education. The African-American leaders, clergy and politicians alike, had mistakenly placed their faith in the federal government to insure that the states would honor their obligation to finally commit the same amount of time and financial resources to educate black children as they had been traditionally doing for white children. These black leaders failed to realize and adequately appreciate the fact that public education is by and large a local government function. Barring the instance of a court order, the education of children, black and white, is primarily the business of local governmental authorities. State and local governments, along with some modest support from the federal level, fund most school districts. As a result the quality of public education is subject to the political agendas of state and local power brokers.

In too many cases the same people who controlled the school districts under segregation, continue to control the districts and set educational goals and policies for black children under desegregation. This is why in virtually every case throughout the south when desegregation finally came to a given school district, all the black high schools were unceremoniously changed to junior high schools and the white high schools became the new high schools in the district. Furthermore, thousands of black high school principals and other black school officials were either demoted or fired as a consequence of this consolidation. Also, this same sinister scenario held true for most of the experienced black teachers. Moreover, even in those integrated schools, with substantially fewer white students, after all of whom could afford it had fled to private schools, were not as well funded as those schools with high white enrollments.

Ironically, this calculated funding discrepancy existed even though both types of schools were located in the same district. This insidious pattern of managed inequality within the same school district later moved to northern cities and throughout the rest of the nation. This is the morally reprehensible duplicity on the part of the educational establishment that accounts for the current sorry state of public education in America today.

When one takes a closer look at exactly what is happening to African-American children in too many school districts across this nation, there can be cause for great alarm! African-American children are being deliberately and systematically tracked into low achieving and unchallenging, non-college preparatory courses of study. When one considers this scandalous duplicity on the part of education officials, coupled with the coldly calculated elimination of African-American teachers from the classrooms, who served as critically important and very tangible role models for black children, it is not difficult to understand why the performance level is so low and dropout rate for black children is so high. Furthermore, when one observes how low the percentage of black teachers really is, in the public educational work force, there is little wonder why black students remain alienated from school and consistently perform poorly on standardized tests. This continues to be the unfortunate reality for black children across this nation. This pathetic state of affairs in American education is tantamount to a scandalous ripoff of African-American children which guarantees that they will grow up to be permanent members of the

74

economic under class. This unspeakably vicious robbery of access to learning and technology which ultimately results in the coldly calculated denial of these children's economic opportunity on the part of the educational establishment is no doubt, the most heinous crime of all. This alone, is reason enough for the African-American church to stand up and re-assert itself as a viable force in the education of African-American children.

Throughout the entire American educational system, there is only one month out of the nine-month educational curriculum in which there is a focus on black history. For the American educational establishment to tell African-Americans that they are so insignificant as a group that they deserve only one month out of nine, to study and observe their contributions to this nation and the world, is down right absurd and absolutely criminal. Implicit in this scandalous verdict, is the notion that African Americans are not as worthy as whites, whose histories are an integral part of the nine-month educational curriculum. This is why the black church must step forward once again, and assume its responsibility as an agent for the proper education of African-American children.

The church could, and definitely should, be a place where people who sincerely care about the true education of African-American children could come and teach them. The church could, and certainly should, be a place where children could not only come to learn about Jesus Christ, but also to learn how to read, write, and count. The church could supplement or expand on what the children are learning in the public schools, especially in those areas of study in which American public education has been criminally negligent. For example, in those areas of traditional African history and culture and African-American history and culture, the church could certainly fulfill that tremendous gap in the educational experience of black children. The church could, and should be the place where African-American children could come and properly learn about their own sexuality, as well as, the moral, ethical, and spiritual responsibility of that sexuality in a psychologically wholesome and spiritually grounded environment. The church could, and should be the place where African-American children and adults could come to learn about proper diet, nutrition, and health and fitness. Moreover, it could be the place where they could be taught how proper diet, and health and fitness could be achieved and maintained within the social and economic context of the African-American experience.

The church could, and should be the place where African-Americans young and old could come and learn how to be the kind of spiritually sound, intellectually ethical, and morally principled, respectable, and responsible men and women that God truly intended. Finally, this eventually will involve an effort of almost supernatural strength because of the backward, ultra conservative, non productive, and tradition shackled leadership now running the church. These white washed tombs with dead men's bones are so entrenched and so averse to doing anything truly constructive for the community that it would literally take a wholesale revolt of revolution-

76

ary dimensions to uproot and remove them. Anything short of a genuine revolutionary revolt by those honest and decent folk who sincerely want to see the church rise up and live out the true meaning of its purpose, will not be sufficient to dislodge the current crop of spiritually dysfunctional, morally clergy who now dominate the leadership of the African-American church.

Martin Luther King showed a glimmer of the church's great potential to organize and mobilize people around certain issues. He was able to organize and galvanize people into an effective mass movement for the achievement of certain rights and privileges of citizenship by bringing tremendous political and economic pressure on government to act. Even King's bitterest opponents realized the importance of the church in the civil rights struggle. That is why so many black churches were bombed and burned by the white terrorists who were determined to keep, "the Nigger in his place". King correctly recognized and wisely appreciated the historical role of the church in the education and mobilization of black people and he sought to harness that spiritual force and make it work for his movement. Therefore, the civil rights movement under the leadership of King was by and large successful in securing for black Americans those citizenship rights which had been denied them for more than a century. Since the unfortunate death of Martin Luther King, the African-American church has not been galvanized anywhere near that extent, as to deal effectively with the myriad of critical and very debilitating issues vexing the African-American community.

I submit that the idea of one month out of the year to focus on the achievements and contributions of African-Americans in the development of this nation was better than nothing at all. However, to continue this practice as if it is sufficient to satisfy the need for the invaluable knowledge of self, especially so sorely lacking among black children, is simply preposterous and absolutely absurd. One month, out of a nine-month school term, to focus study on Blacks, has always been, and continues to be woefully inadequate not only for black children, but for all of America's children. One month, February, which happens to be the shortest month of the year, can only afford enough time for the most scant and cursory survey of Black history. African-American history in America and on the continent of Africa should have long since been integrated into every nine-month public school curriculum in this nation. This should have not only been done for the benefit of black students, but white students too. For they are just as woefully uneducated and misinformed as black children.

The fact that African history is not as an integral component of the educational curriculum for American children as European history, only under-scores the fact that the public education establishment in this nation refuses to truly educate African-American and non-African-American children alike. The fact that information about the contributions of blacks in the development and emergence of America as a world power has not been included in public school curriculums, before integration and has not been included in any significant measure since integration, is compelling evidence that the political

78

power structures throughout this nation have decided not to educate American children. Moreover, the public education policy makers who control the education establishment in America currently are still the very same individuals who controlled it under segregation. This means that African-American children are still being housed in dilapidated schools, with ineffective administrators, poorly trained teachers, and are given an inferior education.

There has been a vast store of valid and credible information about ancient and modern Africa generated by African, as well as non-African scholars during the past 40 years. There has also been a production of volumes of information about the true contributions of African-Americans that have been instrumental in the economic and cultural development of this continent. This critical information, which is crucial to the confirmation of the true identity of our children and the internalization of their ethnic pride and self-confidence, remains by and large locked out of the great majority of public education curricula. This is true even in those school districts supposedly controlled by African-American policy makers. This makes this pathetic situation all the more shameful and tragic. In light of this dismal reality, the African-American church is the last possible hope for truly educating our children and giving them a realistic chance for survival in America.

For the most part, America remains a nation still dominated and controlled by a white power structure built and maintained on the suppression and exploitation of non-white people. Therefore, it is morally incumbent upon the African-American church to rise up and shoulder its responsibility even if it has to be dragged kicking and screaming to this realization. Our survival depends on the black church standing up and being counted as a force for positive change, and moving toward bringing about economic and political empowerment for the African-American community. Rational thinking and morally outraged African-Americans will no longer allow the church to continue to rake in billions of dollars each year, only to provide comfort and luxury for a parasitic clergy class.

Finally, the prospect of the African-American church taking a more active role in the education of its children is no more absurd a notion than the Jewish, Moslem or other religious groups using their synagogues and mosques as vehicles for the spiritual and natural education of their children. I once heard an African-American pastor assert with pompous deliberation, as he stood before the congregation, "I didn't come from Africa. Now maybe some of my ancestors did, but I am not concerned with that. My main concern is Jesus, his having been crucified and his plan of salvation. That is my main concern and all this black history stuff is all right I guess if that is what some people want to focus on, but it is definitely not my thing." I grimaced as I felt a feeling of nausea move over me. Then I felt something akin to despair well up inside of me as I listened to the congregation of mostly middle-aged women and a handful of men voice their sycophantic agreement with such a pitifully misinformed, and tragically misguided soul.

However, this is the grotesquely distorted view of Christianity held by the great majority of African-American pastors. They seemed to have an almost contemptuous attitude toward, and pious disdain for the teaching of anything not straight out of their white washed bibles. Their minds have been so thoroughly white washed with implacable ignorance resulting from generations of racist indoctrination, that they can't even consider the fact that the only accurate and historically valid version of the bible is the story of the African, himself. This tragically pathetic attitude is most pervasive, and deeply entrenched in the African-American church. Even more pathetic, is the arrogant refusal on the part of the majority of the clergy to allow the teaching of information about the role of Africans in the bible. This is the epitome of hypocrisy. The prohibition and outright refusal to teach legitimate and historically validated information with regards to the true role of African characters in the bible is the most grievous injustice and rankest villainy that could possibly be perpetrated by people who claim to be ministers of the gospel. If there is any justice in the universe, and god is the omnipotent judge, then the hottest place in hell will be reserved for those hopeless reprobates, who in His name have purposefully kept the truth from those who have suffered so long, and so much. The truth about the African people has historically been hidden from them by a society that refuses to respect, accept, or appreciate anything black or African.

Finally, without benefit of the rich, in-depth study of the various translations of the Bible, the language used, and how the translation of that language has impacted the modern version of the Bible, the black church is robbed of the full benefit of the vast store of Biblical knowledge. This then illuminates the critical need for the African-American church to rise up, and assert itself as the spiritual beacon of hope and moral example to the community it was intended for. However, the church will never stand up and live up to the true meaning of its purpose until enlightened and brave Christians demand it, by first casting out the legions of blood sucking parasites who are masquerading as leaders. These souls must commit themselves to an honest, sincere, and unadulterated study of Jesus Christ. Moreover, they must ascertain the real significance of His life, and learn how His living example can serve as a model for daily living and how His holy power can serve as a spiritual force for the liberation of the minds and souls of black people. Many Black people are still helplessly lost and wandering aimlessly in the dark wilderness of powerlessness, hopelessness, and self-hatred.

When honest and sincere folk, who have been sitting silent and quiescent under these pimps, punks, and pushers, decide to stand up and strip away the pompous veneer of pious pretension, and demand the teaching of the unadulterated truth, the sad state of affairs in the black church will change. As I have said before, it is no more absurd for African-Americans to use the church as a vehicle for the education of their children, than it is for Jews to use their synagogues, Moslems to use their mosques, or Catholics to use their churches for the education of their children. These religious groups have long since recognized the fact that the public education system would not, and could not teach their children all that they needed to know, to allow them to reach their fullest potential. I have always deeply respected and admired these groups for their determination to take primary responsibility for the most crucial and essential function of educating their own children. This notion of taking care of self and being dedicated to the proposition of all that this notion implies has, unfortunately, not been genuinely embraced by the African-American church. No, I am not saying that we should remove all African-American children from the public schools. On the contrary, keep them there and apply the greatest possible pressure on public education to provide them with all the teaching in science, mathematics, and computer technology that it has made available to others. However, the critical and crucial teaching of ethnic history, the basic concepts of self, self-image, and self-determination must be taught by people who genuinely have the best interest of African-American children at heart. Therefore, I submit that this role could, and should be that of the African-American church. First, it must purge itself of all of those pimps, punks, pushers, and other shuffling handkerchief-head parasites who have done nothing but ruthlessly exploit the African-American community under the guise of religion.

CHAPTER 6

The African-American Church as a Financial Force in the Community

The African-American church establishment with all its various denominations is undeniably the richest institution in the black community. When one considers the vast real-estate holdings, including the church edifices and other related properties, even the most naive mind would be hard pressed to contend that the church does not have the physical facilities to house a viable educational program for its youth. When one considers the urban centers where African-Americans are most heavily concentrated, the landscape is peppered with churches. Throughout rural America where ever African-Americans are in significant numbers, there has historically been, a church presence. When one considers all the churches functioning with varying degrees of support from the surrounding community, it is not difficult to understand the real financial potential lying dormant in the African-American church.

It has been conservatively estimated that the African-American Church, takes in over seven billion dollars a year. Now one must ask the question, where does this money go? What is it really being used for? I contend that, the money has been used and is still being used, to support and maintain a gaudy, ostentatious, and insatiably indulgent clergy class. Much of it has been used, and is still being used to stage lavish church conventions in fancy hotels around the country. Incidentally, none of these hotels are owned or operated by African-Americans. Also, a significant portion of the money is being used to support the construction of larger and more opulent edifices as church congregations frantically compete with each other to scale the heights of gaudy ostentation and regal splendor. As a result, this has created many jobs in the construction industry. Unfortunately, these jobs are almost totally owned and controlled by white construction companies and provide very little real benefit in the way of employment to the surrounding African-American community. The commercial suppliers of church pews, chairs, tables, organs, pianos, and other church paraphernalia and religious materials involved in Christian worship are almost never exclusively supplied by) African-American businesses. Therefore, even the construction and supply of the worship edifices yield virtually no real economic benefits to the congregation or the black community.

These powerfully sobering observations evoke far more provocative questions than they answer. With the number of African-Americans trained in construction and the number of black owned construction companies across the nation, then why hven't more of these black owned construction companies been used to build, or renovate existing black churches? Why hasn't there been greater use of black subcontractors in those church-building projects undertaken by white construction firms? With the unemployment rate of African-American men twice to three times that of white men and black youth unemployment perennially hovering above sixty percent, these questions deserve and demand a sincere response from the church leadership. In light of the unmitigatedly dismal employment prospects for African-American despite their level of education or training, the church can no longer afford to ignore the negative effects of its behavior on the economic status of the black community.

It is reported that one third of all African-American males with college degrees and two thirds of all African-American women with college degrees actually live below the current poverty level. With the current trend of corporate downsizing, corporate mergers, and the frenzied exportation of American jobs overseas, the result has been heightened competition for fewer jobs in a shrinking job market. Consequently, this situation has placed African-Americans, whose employment prospects have always been tenuous at best, because of racism and sexism in corporate America, in an even more precarious predicament. Therefore, the black church must be compelled to take a more honest and ethical look at its own behavior as it relates to the economic health of the African-American community.

For example, if a particular church congregation decides to build a new edifice, it must first do some serious soul searching as to how its building project can best benefit the total community. Is it possible to use an African-American construction company to build the church? Is it possible to secure pews, tables, chairs and other church furnishings from African-

American suppliers? Is it possible to buy choir robes from other African-Americans? Is it possible to buy bibles, hymnals or Sunday school materials from other African-Americans? To the degree that these questions can be answered in the affirmative, it will determine the positive, or negative economic impact that any given church will have on the community. Every one of these endeavors could, and certainly should include and involve other African-Americans in the commercial supply of goods and services to the church. This is precisely how other ethnic groups in this country have been able to develop and expand the economic bases of their communities.

It has been reported that a dollar turns over less than once in the African-American community. Even the most conservative economists agree that it must turn over at least three times before any measurable economic development can take place. Therefore, it is not difficult to understand why the African-American community remains stagnate and stymied while other ethnic groups have managed to continually develop and expand the economic bases of their communities. Studies have shown that African-Americans have an annual income of over three hundred billion dollars. However, ninety-five percent of this income is spent out side of the community. I once heard an African-American preacher explain how he had approached an organization of preachers about the prospect of the churches getting involved in the insurance business. He alluded to, and greatly lamented the fact that so many members of his congregation did not have, and could not afford basic life insurance. He asserted that this troubling situation was widespread throughout the community. Nevertheless, their sanctimonious response to the man was an unequivocal no. They proceeded one after another, to mouth a pathetic litany of pious platitudes about how their job was to save souls. Therefore, they felt that the church had no business being involved in such a secular matter as life insurance. Consequently, the whole matter was permanently tabled by the organization. As a result, the terrible situation of under insured and uninsured people continued, and tragically was regarded by those ministers as a worldly matter outside the purview of the church's leadership. This is a classic example of the backward, non-productive, and reactionary views of the majority of the African-American church leadership. Unfortunately, this view cuts across all denominational lines and it is widespread and deeply entrenched.

This absurdly reactionary philosophy however, has not always been the dominant point of view of the black clergy. On the contrary, the African-American church was once quite active in what lately has been termed, "worldly or secular matters" in the African-American community. I have already said that the black church has played an integral role in the establishment and maintenance of elementary and secondary black schools as well as historically black colleges. Furthermore, the church was once very active in the organization of burial societies, as well as a myriad of other self-help programs designed to support and sustain its membership. I have often heard my mother and her contemporary's talk about the Poor Saints Funds which were an important part of their church operation. This was a church fund supported and maintained by the members of the congregation. It was created for the expressed purpose of assisting members of the congregation and even those in the larger black community who found themselves in need. This genuinely altruistic nature of the early African-American church was the central component of its character. Many are the times that I have sat at my mother's feet and listened to her talk with her friends about the activities of the various women's and men's groups in the church. For example, they would often talk about the prayer circle, the quilting circle, the motherboard, the deacon board, the willing workers, the other church auxiliaries and the status of their various projects in the church and larger community. The church was usually the first place where anyone, who was in need, could turn for help. Moreover, this attitude was encouraged and those seeking help were embraced with the kind of zeal and genuine love and concern that has all but totally disappeared from the great majority of black churches today.

I can remember growing up in rural southeastern Virginia where black churches owned grocery stores, Laundromats, dry cleaners, and all manner of commercial enterprises which provided goods, services and jobs for the general community, as well as for their members. I knew of one church outside of Cleveland Ohio that actually owned a farm with cattle and produced pasteurized milk for sale to the local community. A few decades ago, these kinds of profit making business activities were definitely not uncommon endeavors on the part of many black churches. These kinds of commercial endeavors were not the

89

exception, but the rule for most of them. In a society where black Americans were forced to live under a legally sanctioned apartheid with little or no social welfare support from the government, they realized that the church had to play an essential role in the very survival of the African-American community.

However, with the coming of massive governmental intervention in the form of social welfare programs, the black church has all but totally abandoned its former economic role in the community. As a result, the diminished prominence of the church in the community has in large measure, given rise to the present social disorganization and moral decay which now saturates the African-American community. I submit that the African-American church as a whole must take an honest look at what has happened to the black community over the past five decades. What has been the consequence of its diminished role in the community? What specific factors contributed to its diminished role? Why and how did these factors contribute to its diminished role and give rise to the present situation? A rational analysis of the social, economic and spiritual condition of the African-American community and those internal and external factors which have contributed to these current sorry conditions will take some sincere collective soul searching on the part of the black clergy. I am convinced that it would be an exercise of absolute futility for the average parishioner to hold his or her breath and wait for the church leadership to undertake a rational approach to anything concerning the genuine interest of the black community. Frankly it is not in the clergy's financial interest to do so.

The church's wholesale financial abandonment of the African-American community over the past four decades has been a bonanza for many black preachers. Those financial resources generated by the church which were formerly used to support and sustain the various projects and programs in the church and larger community, now have been siphoned off for the benefit of the preachers and their cronies. As a result, the congregations are being asked to give more and more while the church faithful and the community at large, receive less and less. Unfortunately, this is the prevailing situation in the vast majority of black churches. This reversed Robin Hood philosophy must change. This situation where the many poorer souls are supporting and sustaining a blood sucking, self-indulgent, spiritually dysfunctional few, must be changed. This sickening condition, this ungodly arrangement, can only be corrected when a significant number of the church's faithful, stand up and demand a change. These same faithful few will also have to do their own sincere analysis of the historical role of the church's positive involvement in the black community. Then, they can contrast that situation with the church's financial abandonment of the community in recent decades. As a result, they can but only conclude that the church must again, re-assert itself as a positive spiritual, social, and especially economic force in the community. The current reality demands it and the very survival of the community requires it.

The church, whenever and wherever possible, must provide jobs and wherever it can, and offer job training as part of its construction projects. It must involve African-Americans in an integral way as providers of goods and services in its system of commerce that involves hundreds of millions of dollars a year. This booming business in church construction and remodeling, and the tremendous trade in church furniture, fixtures, bibles, hymnals, choir robes and other biblical study materials, engaged in by black churches, amounts to hundreds of millions of dollars per year. Unfortunately, precious few of the construction dollars are spent with black construction companies, and less than one percent of the trade in other goods and services concerning this multi-million dollar religious enterprise is purchased from other African-Americans. This tragically self-defeating spending philosophy among blacks, which is responsible for the one-way flow of dollars out of the African-American community, must change if any measure of community development is ever going to take place.

There has been much bitter controversy regarding the incidence of non-resident ownership of a large number of the businesses in the African-American community. Most of the African-American anger of late has been directed at individuals of Asian and middle eastern origin who have bought up and now operate, a very significant number of businesses within the black community. The overwhelmingly large number of businesses now owned by these non-residents of the African-American community has been a particularly troublesome problem for many black residents over the past four decades. I have heard reports that in some black communities, upward of 70 percent of the businesses, are owned by non-blacks, and non-residents. However, when a few courageous black leaders have been brave enough to speak out against this dreadfully depressing situation, the larger white society and the foreign business owners alike, of being racist and intolerant, have accused them. However, there has not been a single instance in the entire history of this nation where African-Americans have owned even one percent of the businesses in any other ethnic community, at any time. That situation has simply not been allowed to exist in any other ethnic community in America, except the black community. Nevertheless, when black leaders, do speak out, they are viciously attacked by those, self-serving hypocrites who wouldn't, for one moment, tolerate the same condition to exist in their own communities. Yet, black leaders are excoriated and denounced as being racist and intolerant, for having the audacity to object to this economic rape of their communities.

The phenomenon of non-resident ownership of the majority of the businesses and jobs in the African-American community deserves close analysis. First of all, it is a pathetically tragic fact that major banks and local governments alike throughout this nation have historically played an insidious role in prohibiting the economic development of the black community by the systematic denial of loans and the extension of credit to the residents of those communities. Study after study has revealed the pervasive practice of red lining on the part of many major banks and lending institutions. Furthermore, reports have shown how local governments have actively prohibited the establishment and support of African-American owned businesses through the manipulation of city ordinances such as zoning laws, and other governmental regulations. Reports have revealed that even the

Small Business Administration, a federal program set up ostensibly to assist the establishment and support of small businesses, has not really made a sincere effort in assisting African-Americans with the same kind of financial and technical support that it has historically given to non-blacks. Furthermore, there is the wide spread practice by absentee landlords and other non-black owners of business properties in the black community, of refusing to sell these properties to black residents. Moreover, when non-black, non-resident owners are willing to sell their properties to residents of the community, they demand extremely exorbitant, beyond market prices for them.

As a result, all of these factors have combined to effectively and deliberately lock African-Americans out of the opportunity to establish and develop businesses in their own communities. Meanwhile, white lending institutions and local governments seemed to be tripping over each other to extend credit and dump millions of dollars in loans and credit into the pockets of whites and newly arriving foreigners. This enables them to buy up most of the businesses and then dominate the economies of black communities all over this country. Then, these same local governments and lending institutions simultaneously deny the same loans and credit to African-Americans living in these affected communities.

This malicious under handed shenanigan has served to create bitter feelings and heighten ethnic tensions between African-Americans, Asians, Arabs, Hispanics, and Jews. This unbridled economic exploitation would simply not be allowed to exist, for

94

one second, in any other ethnic community in America. However, it is the unfortunate and pathetic reality in the African-American community. What is even more damnable and absurd is that those few African-American individuals who are courageous enough to voice their disapproval of this condition, are attacked for having these views and accused of being racist and intolerant. I submit that such totally self-serving accusations are nothing but the absolute epitome of hypocrisy on the part of those truly racist demagogues who have the unmitigated audacity to excoriate others, for having the nerve to voice their objection to these economically deleterious conditions existing in the African-American community.

In light of these dismal conditions and this very sobering reality, the African-American church must ask itself, now what is the plan and where do we start? First of all, Black churches must re-learn the value of cooperative effort. African-American Christians do more talking about unity, and actually show less of it than any other ethnic or religious group in this country. There is absurdly little serious cooperation on any substantive issue among black churches even within the same denominations. This must be reversed if any genuine progress is ever to be made. Even if those churches within the same denominations could learn to trust and cooperate with each other on serious social and economic projects that benefit the entire community, the impact would be immediate and tremendous. For example, a few months ago, I was listening to a fellow Christian complain about how difficult it was becoming to buy airtime on a local secular radio station for their church programming. I asked why some of these black churches did not pool their money and buy their own radio station? They would then have a medium to air their church programming and have total control over the presentation of that programming. For a moment the individual was silent, then he spoke, "Yeah, that is right, we should get together and do something like that." Unfortunately that was the end of the discussion and for all intents and purposes, the end of the idea. This is virtually always the case when there is any suggestion of doing anything constructive in the black church.

What if it had not been the end of the discussion and we were able to bring it before the monthly meeting of the Ministerial Alliance? What if five of the thirty-four member churches had thought it was a grand idea and had decided to move forward with it at once? What if the pastors of these five churches which had answered in the affirmative, had gone enthusiastically back to their congregations and sold them on the idea? What if these five churches had resolved to do this thing, and forged ahead pooling their money and making plans to acquire a radio station? I submit that the closer this group moved toward the actual accomplishment of this goal, the more other churches who had initially turned down the idea, would have found themselves reversing their former stance and coming into the fold. This is how easy it would be to accomplish the acquisition of a Christian radio station, by people who know how to work together

This same scenario can apply to the purchase of any other commercial entity. Let's say that two or

96

three church congregations came together and purchased a grocery store. First, jobs would be created for the members. Secondly, if the members of the congregations involved resolved that they would buy all their groceries at this particular store there would be a guaranteed customer base. Therefore, the probability of the store's commercial success would be virtually guaranteed. This would stimulate a measure of pride and genuine feeling of self-determination which could definitely become contagious, and quickly spread throughout the whole African-American community.

Furthermore, it would certainly serve as a powerfully tangible example in the community for other churches to duplicate. The church can no longer afford to stand passively on the side line in sanctimonious complacency holding its purse strings tightly, except when it come to lavishing financial appreciation on the clergy, while the community sinks deeper and deeper into poverty, and hopelessness. At a time when other religious organizations are amassing tremendous amounts of commercially viable and employment producing businesses for their congregations, the African-American church remains almost totally unconcerned with the sorry economic condition of the community. Therefore, the black church must be challenged to get up from its sanctimonious stool of do-nothingism and accept its moral and economic responsibility to its faithful and the larger community. Black Christians have to eat, sleep, wear clothes, shoes, use soap, detergent, toothpaste, toilet paper, and have the same material needs as everyone else. Now it is high time that they realized that they must become providers of many of these goods and services for each other. It is totally asinine for African-American Christians to continue to perpetuate this one way flight of dollars out of their community while other religious groups are busy maximizing their financial potential by boldly moving into business opportunities and creating gainful employment for their members. So while the African-American clergy sit around in its stiff-necked piety, clinging tenaciously to its reactionary philosophy of religious abstinence from anything to do with the improvement of the material existence of the faithful, other religious groups are acquiring vast tracts of farm land, fleets of ships, and making major inroads into manufacturing and service industries. There are many non-African-American Christian churches that own radio and television stations, supermarkets, restaurants, hospitals, hotels, clothing stores, and all manner of commercial enterprises which provide good paying jobs for their members. These religious groups came to the realization long ago, that it was also an essential part of their function as churches in their communities to provide some means of economic survival for their members.

This same critical economic realization was also once acknowledged and embraced by the historical black church. One only needs to do a cursory survey of its economic activity in the black community prior to the 1950's to see how deeply it was involved. After the 1950's, the black church lost its economic way on the road to integration and assimilation into the larger white society. The church's historical philosophy of self-reliance was unceremoniously discarded in favor of a myriad of government sponsored social welfare programs. Now however, we are all, the worst off for it. In light of the present dismal economic, moral, and spiritual condition of the black community, it is imperative that the church resurrects this lost philosophy of self-reliance and self-determination. It must once again, make this crucial philosophy an integral part of its function in the community. There are all kinds of examples of how this can be accomplished as has been exhibited by other religious groups all over America. Therefore, there is no excuse for claiming ignorance and no defense for doing nothing.

Obviously, the African—American church cannot be expected to solve the entire myriad of deleterious problems vexing the black community, but it certainly can solve some of them. It definitely has the financial wherewithal and the potential to make a tremendous economic impact on the community. The only things that are lacking are the black clergy's honesty to acknowledge the existence of these pervasive problems, the courage to accept its responsibility to address them, and the determined will to act. Then however, the issue becomes a question of morality. What is the morally appropriate thing to do? What is the ethical responsibility of the church to its faithful and the larger community? How can it best address the true spiritual and material needs of the faithful, and reach out to the larger community? Once these questions have been dealt with honestly and forthrightly in the context of true Christian love and sincerity, the implementation of a self-help program, on the part of the black church, would be simply a matter of course.

Again, it is the grandest folly to expect the present leadership of the African-American church establishment to even consider these questions with anything approaching genuine sincerity or true Christian love. They are part and parcel of the problem. Furthermore, the great majority of them are perfectly satisfied with the way that things already are. They are already more than amply provided for. They are already perched comfortably at the top of the present parasitic relationship between the congregation and the clergy. They are more than satisfied with this perverse arrangement and cannot be expected to disturb the status quo. Therefore, the job of researching the historical record of the black church's economic activity in the community, and its former prominence in the life of black folk, will certainly fall to the faithful in the congregation and not the clergy.

The silent majority of the faithful that know in their collective hearts, that something is dreadfully wrong with the black church, will have to stand up and demand this kind of positive change because it will not, and cannot come from the present church leadership. A reactionary black clergy, for the most part, has been the major obstacle to any meaningful spiritual, moral, and especially economic development in the community on the part of the church. They have simply not been up to the challenge for so critical and crucial a job. Moreover, the black clergy, in its spiritually brain-dead and morally gelded message, along with perpetuating its profound ignorance of the natural and spiritual truths, has also exacerbated and compounded an already pathetic situation for the black church faithful.

CHAPTER 7

The Segmentation of the African-American Church

"One God, One Faith, and One Baptism." *Eph. 4: 5.* If there is one aspect of life in the African-American community where it would be possible to obtain a strong consensus about what is right or wrong, it could be religion. The central message of the Christian bible asserts that the true believers have a commonality of perception and a shared value system, based on a single standard of behavior. Consequently, Christians are commanded to live in accordance with the dictates of the scriptures and be guided by a singleness of purpose as exemplified by the life of Jesus Christ. The Bible declares that the primary tenants of the Faith, as delineated in the Ten Commandments should be reflected in the daily lives of all who profess to be disciples of Jesus Christ. Jesus Christ declared: "the world will know that ye are my disciples by the love that ye show one to another". *John 13: 35.* In other words, he was saying that attitude and behavior would be the primary standard by which the world would know who the Christians are. In fact, his true disciples would be just like him. The bible exalts, encourages, and implores believers to come to the unity of the faith and the oneness of God's divine purpose. However, herein lies the main problem. It is the way that the bible has been interpreted.

The interpretation of the bible has been construed by religious demagogues over the centuries in a way that seeks to rationally justify, and morally accommodate various exploitative political and economic philosophies that have had nothing whatsoever to do with Christianity. The bible has been used to justify some of the most savage and sadistic crimes ever committed by one ethnic group against another in the annals of human history. These atrocities have range from the crimes of the Crusades, to the African slave trade, to the Jewish holocaust. The Bible has been used in the malicious attempt to stereotype and vilify Jews as, "Christ killers". This was done in order to consolidate and crystallize the malignantly racist dogma which justified the merciless degradation of, and discrimination against Jews all over the world. Similarly, the bible has been used in an attempt to justify African slavery by demonizing and vilifying the black man as sub-human, and biologically more akin to the ape than to white ethnics. Furthermore, according to white racist pseudo-Christian dogma, the African has been called the cursed son of Ham.

As a result, he has been thus relegated to eternal servitude at the pleasure of Jafat and Chim, and their children's children, meaning all of the light complexioned or white European ethnics. This preposterous, malevolent, and malignant racial myth has been promoted for centuries as legitimate Biblical scripture. Moreover, it has actually been used to suggest that God ordained North American slavery, himself. This malignant myth has been vigorously promoted from one generation to the next by racist Europeans,

102

and became their primary justification for African slavery and the subsequent barbaric treatment of black Americans during, and since slavery.

Therefore, it has been this wickedly perverse interpretation of the bible that has been the sadistic justification for the savage brutality and ruthless barbarity perpetrated for centuries, against the black man in particular, and other people whom so called "white Christian" Europeans have classified as non-white, non-Western peoples all over the globe. This manipulation of the bible has persisted unabated down through countless generations, and it remains just as tragic in its effect today. Ironically, this same carnal-minded, lowlife manipulation of the bible is just as pervasive in the African-American church. The evidence of this incipient phenomenon is overwhelming and speaks very loudly.

One needs only to observe the pervasive segmentation, factionalism and ungodly rivalries that have splintered the black church body over the years. Further evidence of this insidious manipulation of the bible is the proliferation and influence of the pimp, punk, and pusher preachers along with other skilled religious demagogues with intentions just as perverse and despicable. "My ways are as different from your ways as the heavens are above the earth, and my thoughts are as different from your thoughts as the east is from the west." *Isaiah 55:8-9*. The scriptures clearly delineate how vastly different a sinful and carnal mind is from that Holy and eternally divine mind. Therefore, the scripture asserts in Christ's own words, " I am the true vine and he who abide in me shall be a branch that shall bring forth

103

much fruit." *John 15:5-7.* I submit that this is the unequivocal affirmation that it is impossible to know the mind of God unless His spirit is living in one. Jesus Christ said, "It is needful that I go away so that the comforter can come. He will lead and guide you into all righteousness and perfect my will in you." *John 16:7*

The problem for centuries has been that men and women have endeavored to interpret the bible based on their own carnal minded, self-centered understanding, and selfish motivations which have been anything but Christian. They have taken their own carnal philosophies and tried to manipulate the scriptures in a way that the bible would support and buttress their own view of the world. More wars have been waged and more carnage, death and destruction have been wrought in the name of religion than any other reason. This has been the result of man's own selfish, carnal, perverse, and patently self-serving interpretation of the bible. Christianity or what many people call Christianity has been so segmented, fractionalized, and balkanized that instead of promoting tolerance and acceptance, it has promoted contempt, competition, and prejudice. Moreover, and perhaps even more tragic, instead of truly liberating the minds and hearts of people with the honest teaching of the real historical and spiritual Jesus Christ, the bible has been used to deceive, diminish, and enslave the minds of men and women all over the globe. I submit that this carnal minded attempt to interpret the Bible, (according to one's own selfish world view), has yielded results just as disastrous in the African-American community.

The result of this manipulation and self-serving interpretation of the Bible has been a devastating obstacle to any hope of genuine unity in the black church. Conversely, it has merely promoted wholesale segmentation, factionalism and denominational rivalry in the African-American church. This has made the entire church body tremendously weak and impotent over the years. It has become an exercise in utter futility for even the most brilliant mind to try and reconcile all of these various and divergent interpretations of the bible with the idea of "One God, one faith, and one baptism". *Eph. 4:4-6.* This mass confusion in Christendom, as a result of this grotesquely carnal minded interpretation of the scriptures, has severely weakened the total influence of the church and greatly crippled its ability to generate any semblance of a true consensus or spirit of genuine unity in the faith.

However, a precious few enlightened members of the black clergy have begun to recognize the terribly destructive effects of these distorted interpretations of the bible and are beginning to move away from this ludicrous factionalism and denominational segmentation. They have come to realize how counter-productive and divisive these artificial barriers which have been erected over the years, are to the promotion of true Christian unity. As a result, a few brave and progressive souls among the clergy are trying to counter these deleterious effects wrought by denominational division. These artificial barriers, erected over the years by denominational dogma, have been some of the fundamental reasons why the African-American church has been so thoroughly segmented, fractionalized, and hopelessly divided. This division has severely limited the black church's spiritual and economic potential in the community as a whole. These denominational divisions have made it virtually impossible for the African-American church to unite around a specific agenda. Furthermore, these denominational divisions seem to create and encourage more conflict and competition than anything resembling cooperation. Therefore, religious demigods, who have consistently put their own selfish interests ahead of that of the church's faithful and that of the larger community, have basically destroyed the element of unity which has historically been the primary source of strength of the black church. This is the real tragedy of the African-American church in America. This is why I contend that its power is still only potential and has in no way been fully realized.

There is a small group among the clergy who appear to have realized the great potential of a united church and they are moving toward a non-denominational church. This group is small and there are members within it who are not willing to conform to the dictates of any specific denomination. Unfortunately, even among these, there are still some, who are not interested in uniting with anybody, for any reason. So, even among the very best and brightest of the black clergy, there are some vicious wolves dressed in sheep's clothing. Yet, among this group, there are those who have to be separated from those who are genuinely concerned with, and striving for, a united church.

Another problem that compounds denominational divisions is the high incidence of serious philosophical differences, even within a given denomination. The particular nuances of style, idiosyncrasies of presentation and the level of self- indulgence of the particular pastor with regards to his interpretation of the denominational view of the bible will all impact on the religious outlook and orientation of any given church. The religious party line for lack of a better term is, established by the particular pastor in any given church. Even his own personal opinions about things not specifically covered in the scriptures still tend to carry the same weight as his opinion about scripture in his or her church. There is no consensus even within the same denominations on issues like appropriate dress, the use of instrumental music, and whether or not women are allowed in the pulpit. The parishioners for the most part, will invariably adopt the same attitudes as the pastor regarding these matters. Many members of the clergy seem to search for things that divide and factionalize the church when such an approach is necessary to suit their own personal agendas. These pimps, punks and pushers along with other pseudo- religious demagogues have consistently perverted the gospel to support their own selfish ends. This wicked perversion of the true gospel of Jesus Christ must be challenged if the church is ever going to be what God intended for it to be.

Those honest and decent folk, sincerely seeking to do the will of God, must watch and pray. Furthermore, the scriptures implore the faithful to "Study to show thy self-approved unto God". I submit that in order to combat those reprobates who are able to deceive the faithful and shamelessly exploit them, one must get an understanding of the word for him-

or herself. John 8:31-36: One must sincerely accept Jesus Christ as Lord and Savior, and His Holy Spirit which will lead and guide the true believer into all truth and righteousness. The divinely lucid mind can only be achieved through Holy living and the spiritual light of eternal truth. For it is this God-centered mind that can rightly divide the Word of Truth and expose those hollow hypocrites for what they really are. It is more critical now, in these last days, that the church move toward a unity in the faith. With the skyrocketing escalation of crime, vice, aids, teenage pregnancy, joblessness, and hopelessness in the African-American community, the church can no longer afford to stand idly by in sanctimonious complacency and do nothing but provide jobs for preachers. If the current church leadership cannot see the dire need for church unity, or feel the spiritual imperative for a unity of the faith, they are deaf, dumb, and blind, or they simply do not care. In any event, they should be removed. They have for too long, been a part of the problem that has fostered the current pathetic condition of the African-American church.

It is going to take genuine Christian love and unity which can only be borne out of the kind of spiritual oneness engendered by the Holy Spirit. This in dwelling of the Holy Spirit will not happen until, or unless, there is an honest repentance for sin, and a genuine acceptance of Jesus Christ as Lord and Savior. Furthermore, there must be a sincere effort to obey his will. "How will the world know that ye are my disciples? - By the love that you show one for the other.". *John 13:35*. It is this kind of unity that I am talking about; the kind of Christian love and unity that can bind men and women together as true spiritual brothers and sisters. This is the kind of Christian unity that will allow the church to reach consensus with regard to Christian values which could produce a single standard for righteous behavior, and allow the church to speak with one definitive voice concerning what is right and what is wrong. That definitive voice will also agree on what is good and what is evil, what is morally appropriate and what is morally inappropriate. This kind of unity could finally enable the black church to speak with one voice and act in one accord. It is this kind of Christian unity that could motivate the church to maximize its collective strength and realize its full spiritual and economic potential. Finally, it is this kind of genuine Christian love and unity that would inspire the church to educate African-American children and provide them with the true knowledge of their heritage, in Africa as well as here in America. Furthermore, it is this kind of true Christian love and unity that could compel the church to become a positive and productive economic force, by being a provider of jobs and hope for the millions of young African-American who are without either. It is this kind of true Christian love and unity, and only this kind of love and unity that could truly galvanize the African-American church and transform it into a force for positive change in the community.

It is going to take love, which can only be realized through a life totally committed to Christ and the strength of true Christian unity, in order for the church to have the power to grapple with the myriad of maladies now affecting the African-American community. Do not expect this movement to come from the present clergy. It will of necessity, be a grass roots movement because the clergy is so much a part of the prevailing problem, that it cannot offer any legitimate solutions. It has all but lost credibility within the community. It has lost too much of its former moral suasion and its ability to influence the community because of its constant misuse of its moral authority. This is why this movement, if it is to bring about unity of the faith, must be led by those folk who have not been tainted and corrupted by the current leadership in the black church. It must be raised up, and led by people who are committed to, and led by the real historical and spiritual Jesus Christ. Those people who have been born again, and have the Holy Spirit of Christ living in them can only undertake the movement. These must be people who have consistently demonstrated by their actions, that they have the love of God in their hearts. They must be people who cannot watch the suffering of their own children and do nothing. They must be people who cannot bear to watch the withering pain and utter despair their youth and not try to heal it. They cannot view the utter hopelessness of their own community and not try to remedy it. Those who cannot see this as the primary charge of the Christian church and be moved with compassion to act will merely remain more a part of the problem than any meaningful part of the solution. Therefore, again I submit that the most important qualification for this kind of dedicated Christian service is the genuine acceptance of Jesus Christ as one's personal Lord and Savior. Jesus said," I am the true vine, and he who abides in me, I will abide in him." *John 15:1.* Outside of this intimate relationship with Christ, it would be literally impossible to fulfill the true mission of the church in the community.

The real problems affecting the black community, never seem to get addressed simply because there are too many folk in church leadership positions, who don't have a clue as to who the historical or spiritual Jesus Christ really is, nor do they have the slightest intention of ever finding out. They have never known, and have no inkling of the actual power and glory of God because they have never truly accepted him as their own personal Lord and Savior. Largely people, who in deed have a form of godliness but deny the power thereof, lead the black Church. *II Tim. 3:5* They bellow lofty platitudes about the power of God and pontificate endlessly about His mighty hand but yet they are afraid to trust Him enough to actually step out on their faith in the authority of His power. They deny the power of his authority by their very faithlessness and hypocrisy. *II Tim. 3:1-7.* This is why there has been no real effort on the part of the church to grapple with the problems confronting the African-American community.

The problems troubling Black Christians are those same problems vexing the larger black community. The leadership simply doesn't have the faith in God or the confidence in itself as believers, to act in any courageous and constructive manner to address these problems. I reiterate, that those Christians who are moved by the genuine love of God and true Christian compassion to positive action, will ultimately have to be in the vanguard of such a spiritually revolutionary change. "Do good unto all men, especially those of the household of faith." *Gal. 6: 10*. It is with this vision, and this compassion, and commitment, that the church will rise up and fulfill its true mission and purpose in the African-American community. Anything less than this genuine Christian approach grounded in the love of Jesus Christ and led by His spirit will result in more of the same shenanigans that we already have: deception, exploitation and utter hopelessness.

Finally, the church certainly could, and by all means should, be an important economic force in the African-American community. It has tremendous potential to provide jobs for its faithful as well as employment opportunities for the larger community. It is time for the church to start involving the community in its commercial trade. It has, for too long, provided jobs for people outside of the community. The black church has consistently exported its wealth to other communities while its own community sinks deeper and deeper into poverty and hopelessness. Here are just a few examples of the kinds of job producing commercial enterprises that churches could get involved with and virtually guarantee a measure of success: a small or medium sized grocery store, a gas station, an auto repair shop, a clothing store, a Laundromat, a dry cleaning store, a drug store, a shoe store, a furniture store, a flower shop, a child care center, and a radio station. These are just a few commercial businesses that could definitely provide decent paying jobs for members of the church congregation and certainly would bring a real sense of pride back to the community.

All the teaching on purely spiritual things will not satisfy the souls of men if they cannot see how it can be applied to the physical and natural world in which they have to live. Men want to know, and be shown by living example, exactly how the church's message can help them to feed, clothe, and house their families. Therefore, the church must come to grips with the fact that man is flesh as well as spirit and the needs of the spirit cannot be addressed, unless the needs of man's physical existence are also honestly addressed. So this is the total unadulterated mission of the church and its divine purpose on this earth. None but those who have truly accepted Jesus Christ as their personal Lord and Savior, and are led by His Holy Spirit, are equipped and qualified by Him, to do His will on this earth. So, to follow anyone who is not truly being led by the spirit of Jesus Christ will result in nothing but frustration and disillusionment.

CHAPTER 8

Problems and Prescriptions

Given the fact that the black church is the only institution in America over which African-Americans exercise some measure of effective control, it has attracted all manner of charlatans, rascals and religious demagogues. These individuals have systematically prostituted the gospel and subverted the true mission of the church in order to achieve their own selfish ends. The pimps, punks, and pushers are some of the more extreme examples of this unsavory element that has been so entrenched in the black church. They have endeavored to fleece the flock with the rankest form of religious exploitation. As a result, millions and millions of African-Americans living in abject poverty, and utter hopelessness have been fed a steady diet of this gilded gospel. It is a grotesquely dubious message that seeks to sanctify their poverty and justify their hopelessness. It does this by telling them that, "It will all be over after a while." This kind of audacious subterfuge and pseudo-sanctimony has been incredibly successful in duping millions of impoverished souls, with the promise of milk and honey in the "Hereafter", who were seeking a way out of their sorry circumstances in the "Here and Now".

These people are led to believe that it is holy to live in poverty, while the perpetrators of this fraud reli-

114

gion live in regal splendor. As a result, those empty-hearted and morally bankrupt parasites have seized the reigns of leadership in the church, claiming that God called them. However, in reality, these scandalous reprobates have been the black church's worst enemies. Those who have masqueraded as shepherds of the flock and preachers of the gospel have in fact been the most insatiable exploiters of the very people that they purport to serve.

Many of these unscrupulous characters have entered politics and used the church as a means to that end. They have not only used the church as a platform for launching their own political careers, but some of them have used their influence as pastors to barter the votes of their congregations for economic favors from the political power elite. This situation on its face is pathetic enough: however it becomes even more despicable when it is obvious that the votes of the congregation are usually bargained away for a seat on some commission, board, or political appointment to some governmental agency which directly benefits no one, except these preachers and their cronies. I stated at the outset of this chapter, that the black church is the only institution in this society that is primarily controlled by African-Americans. However, it is still indirectly dominated by the influence of the larger white Christian church establishment.

Its version of the gospel is virtually indistinguishable from that of the larger white church. In other words, the black church has embraced the same spiritually brain-dead, morally gelded, and hopelessly corrupt version of the gospel that sanctioned chattel slavery and justified the sadistic dehumanization of the African. This is the same perverse version of Christianity which views black folk as the cursed children of Ham and relegates them to the status of servants of the white ethnics. *Genesis 9:18-27.* There is a story in the book of Genesis which alleges that his father cursed Ham, one of the sons of Noah. According to the story, Noah had gotten drunk from wine and fallen asleep naked in his tent. Upon entering the tent and seeing his father in such a shameful state, Ham was supposed to have laughed at him, and then went and told his other two brothers what he'd seen. However, they were not amused and did not find what Ham had told them funny. They went to their father's tent and covered his nakedness, being careful not to look upon him in such a shameful state. So when Noah awoke from his drunken stupor and learned how Ham had laughed at him, he was enraged and cursed Ham. The story also implies that Noah was violently angry because he realized that his own son, Ham, had sodomized him while he was naked, drunk, and helpless. In any event, Ham was cursed and the curse was placed upon his children's children for generations.

This myth, concocted by certain so called biblical scholars and attributed to the authorship of Moses as legitimate scripture, has been the object of great suspicion by African-American scholars for years. Europeans have conveniently used this malignant myth as justification for the most savage and sadistic treatment of black people for centuries. This version of Christianity which was used to justify, and condone such sadistic wickedness, is the version of the bible that is used in one hundred percent of the white churches in America today. Furthermore, it is used in nearly the same percentage of black churches too. However, over the years, many European, so-called Biblical scholars, have tried to free their countrymen from their shame and guilt for their bottomless savagery against the African, by asserting that the enslavement of the black man was actually ordained by God. They pompously declared that the enslavement of the black man was the divine will of God because the African was a sub-human creature living as a primitive savage, isolated from the rest of the world, living on a dark, backwards, and mysterious continent. Therefore, it was God's will that the "Christian" Europeans remove him from his base existence in Africa and lift him to an acceptable level of human civilization by enslaving him and indoctrinating and Christianizing him with the civilizing influences of Western Culture.

This indelibly racist mentality remains extremely potent, deep-seated, and is still all-pervasive in western culture today. It is the real reason why America has remained primarily since its inception, two societies: one black and restricted to a racial cast, the other white and free. The African has been almost totally written out of the scriptures. However, even in those instances where he appears, his presence has been minimized, marginalized, and rendered insignificant. The white religious establishment has historically declared that the black man and his blackness have been a divine curse and therefore something to be rejected, reviled, feared, and despised. Furthermore, its version of the Bible asserts that the

African and his kind are fit only to be drawers of water and hewers of wood and eternal servants to the lighter skinned Europeans. This distorted version of Christianity is replete with the same racist dogma that was created by western Europeans to vilify the black man so that they could redefine him as sub-human chattel in order to justify their subsequent four hundred years of African enslavement.

The European masters imposed a kind of systematic domination over the African slave that stripped him of every vestige of his language, religion, history, and culture, which left him totally disconnected from his motherland and completely alienated from his natural black African self. In other words, the African slave in North America was left homeless and culturally naked before the world. He had been kidnapped from his home in Africa and cast into a psychological no-man's land of ethnic amnesia and cultural schizophrenia: he was neither African, nor American. Furthermore, this same perverse version of Christianity has been used to enslave the African psychologically, by convincing him that God ordained his enslavement. Therefore, he should quiescently submit to his master and accept his bondage. Also, the Western European version of Christianity has been in lock step with the racist pseudo-scientific dogma that contends that the black man is innately inferior to white people and is considered the least worthy branch of the human family.

Given the nature of the culture that produced these characters that came and prostituted the gospel and exploited the people, it is not difficult to understand why conditions in the black church are in such a sorry state. Furthermore, given the distorted, convoluted, and patently specious version of the bible used by the white church establishment which is the same vaunted version that has been embraced and deified by the black church, one can begin to grasp the root causes of the black church's pathetically tragic dilemma. The consequence of being socialized into, and indoctrinated by a culture which rejects and despises the African and his culture to the point of suggesting that he is innately inferior to other human beings, has undoubtedly psychologically traumatized an spiritually scandalized an entire ethnic group. Consequently a religion which fosters such vitriolic and profoundly negative beliefs about his motherland and culture, only heightens the black man's sense of psychological and emotional alienation from his African ethnicity and natural black African self. These are the two most critical and compelling reasons why those parasitic leaches that have rushed forward to seize the reigns of leadership in the black church must be removed at all cost. They and their warped view of the gospel, handed down to them by their slave masters, must be excised from the African-American church body if its spiritual, moral, and economic health is ever going to be realized.

These unprincipled, unscrupulous and immoral characters have embraced and internalized every negative trait and value forced on the African-American by the larger society. For example, the practice of denominational rivalry, the haughty contempt for any form of intra-church cooperation, and the inability to produce any credible plan of economic cooperation and mobilization have all combined to render the black church hopelessly ineffective and totally obsolete as an economic force or instrument for positive economic empowerment in the community. Furthermore, its hostile rejection of any religious point of view different from its own has resulted in a black church that is divided, disorganized and impotent. Consequently, those values and traits such as cooperation, organization, coalition, and compromise which are essential to enable the black church to fulfill its spiritual mission and economic purpose in the African-American community, are absent. They are actually viewed with bitter sarcasm and utter contempt and therefore pushed aside in favor of the disruptive, disjointed, and disorganized approach which has yielded nothing but chaos and disillusionment. This is why those servile lackeys, calling themselves leaders, must be removed. Furthermore, their destructive and grossly distorted version of Christianity must be abandoned. We must change the actors and the script for a new historically valid and spiritually sound interpretation of the bible. We must take the time and effort to engage in diligent research and rational analysis of the scriptures and understand how they originated and how they have been grossly manipulated and distorted over the centuries.

Finally, we must confront our own profoundly destructive sense of racial inferiority. This has been a culturally engendered sense of racial inferiority that we couldn't help but internalize because we, African-Americans, are all products of this racist culture. It is simply illusory to try to deny the fact that we have not been deeply stained and tainted by our socialization as products of western culture, and members of this society. Just as white Americans have been fundamentally and profoundly molded psychologically by the basic values, beliefs, and traditions of this culture with the notion that they are naturally superior to blacks. We, black Americans, have been similarly molded by those very same forces of culture and shaped by those fallacious notions of our innate inferiority to whites. This is that deathless monster that lives in the psyche, or subconscious mind of every single black man and woman who has been born and raised in a land dominated and controlled by white Western European Culture. It is precisely this deathless and diabolical fiend that sinks its fangs into the very core of our psyches and wreaks havoc on our spiritual and mental health. It has all but paralyzed us intellectually, crippled us psychologically, and immobilized us spiritually. Furthermore, it has robbed us of our self-esteem and self-confidence and left us pathetic and fawning after those who have nothing but pity or contempt for us. Yet we are left with a pathetic determination to pursue them and continue to beg them to recognize us and plead for them to affirm or validate us as fellow human beings. So it is this hideous and deathless monster, that dwells in the inner sanctum or psyche of every black man and woman, that we must confront and ultimately destroy if there is ever to be a chance for true psychological health and wholeness. This is something that every one of us, who hopes to attain anything approaching real mental health, must do before we are ever going to realize our potential, and assume our places in this world as rational and free thinking men and women. Moreover, we must challenge and explode the myth of white superiority in every aspect of American life. It is just as vital to the mental health of white people that they also, confront and ultimately slay that psychological monster which, likewise, lurks deep in their collective psyche and just as thoroughly robs them too, of their own spirituality and humanity.

Those white people who cannot face, and ultimately deal effectively with, the reality that they have been raised on the ridiculously pathetic myth of their innate superiority to all darker skinned people, will forever be just as intellectually dishonest, emotionally crippled, and psychologically dysfunctional as we are. The fact that so many white Americans are infected with the irrational belief in the notion that they are actually inherently superior to black people in particular and all darker skinned people in general, accounts for their deep-seated fear and inexpiable hatred of black folk. This psychological need to actually believe that they are innately superior to darker skinned people has become such an essential component of most white people's basic identity, that they have become mentally, emotionally, and spiritually dysfunctional. They will never be able to have normal relationships with black folk, based on mutual respect and equality, because such an option is totally outside of their frame of reference due to the mass insanity imposed on them as a consequence of their indoctrination into Western European Culture. Consequently, they have been taught from the cradle that the black man is their ultimate physical nemesis and psychological boogieman. Therefore, according to this age-old and grotesquely distorted perception, the black man is the primary source of all of their

122

problems and the object of their most vitriolic hatred and worst possible fears.

Ironically, the larger white society tells us black folk to forget about what has happened in the past, after all, history is really not all that important. The great majority of white Americans concede that even though slavery was a horrible institution, white people living today had nothing to do with it. Therefore, they are neither guilty, nor responsible for what their forefathers did to black people. They lament our insistence on dredging up the past because they contend it only makes us bitter and hostile toward them. So in the interest of racial harmony and integration we should just look to the future and forget about our painful past. I submit that unfortunately, this is the specious argument that far too many African-Americans have already bought into for the illusive sake of racial harmony. The worst possible thing that we can do is to forget about our splendid past which includes thousands of years of our existence on the African continent, centuries before the advent of North American slavery.

Also, we should learn everything about the institution of North American slavery and our sojourn in this nation. We still don't really know how extremely important and virtually indispensable the black man's role actually was in the economic, industrial, and scientific development of this nation. Until very recently, most of the information about the black man's role in the development of America had been, carefully and deliberately, omitted from the history books. Herein lies the genesis of our present problems as a people living on the North American continent. I submit that the truth about our role in the building of this nation, and somewhere in the dynamics of that savage and sadistic system of human slavery, lye the answers that could set us on the path to psychological wholeness. We must first resolve to be resolute in our determination to understand how, and why, men and women had to be stripped of their humanity by the systematic elimination of their language, religion, and Culture in order to make them chattel.

Furthermore, we must carefully analyze and gain a thorough understanding of how the component parts of the political, social, and economic philosophies of Western Europe was translated into a body of racist dogma in order to permit so-called civilized men to commit such unspeakably heinous crimes against a whole group of human beings. Although the institution of slavery is no longer with us, the same racist dogma that was created to justify and facilitate it remains intact as an inextricable and fluid part of western culture. This view of black people as sub-human and being naturally inferior to whites still permeates the fabric of Western European Culture and invariably shapes all attitudes and governs all conscience and unconscious behavior of everyone under its influence. Furthermore, those same age old racist myths of white superiority and black inferiority are still prominently interlaced like quilt stitching throughout the ethnic patchwork, that is the fabric of American society and western culture. Consequently, they invariably and profoundly color the perception, shape the attitudes, and influence the behavior of all Americans, black, red, yellow, brown, and white, in

124

such a profoundly negative way that few of them are willing to admit, even to themselves.

There is general consensus among even western psychologists that an effective therapy for those suffering as adults from certain forms of neuroses often lies in the examination of painful childhood experiences. I submit that black Americans have been psychologically traumatized as a group by the institution of slavery and therefore must confront and ultimately deal with those painful experiences before we can move forward in any healthy, constructive, and self-actualizing way. Therefore the church, being the only institution in this society that the African-American can shape and influence in his own self-interest, is the logical place to start. Those decent and honest men and women who sincerely want the church to reflect the character of Jesus Christ and carry out his mission here on earth, must stand up and step forward. The black church could, and should, be reformed and perhaps redefined all together in order to truly fulfill its mission of saving souls and then teaching those souls how to enjoy the abundant life that God has promised them here on this earth. Can this be accomplished? Yes, but it is going to take a lot of doing, just as anything truly worth while does.

There must be at the outset, a clear understanding that there is going to be tremendous opposition, especially from the current entrenched and reactionary leadership, to this kind of change. Furthermore, there will no doubt, be many casualties of good folk in this struggle. However, you can take heart because your victory will ultimately come. A lie can't stand forever, because the moral arc of the universe is long but it bends towards truth and justice. Moreover, because God said, "No weapon formed against you shall prosper and all those who rise up against His people shall fall". So if you are sincerely seeking the truth that God said, "Shall make you free", you must first, get an understanding of who the true historical and spiritual Jesus Christ is. *Proverbs 4:7*. "Then you must put on the whole armor." *Ephesians 6:14-18*. "Then having your loins gird about with truth, and having on the breast plate of righteousness," *Verse 15*; "and your feet shod with the preparation of the gospel and peace," *Verse 16*; "Above all, taking the shield of faith, where with ye shall be able to quench all the fiery darts of the wicked", *Verse 17*; "And take the helmet of salvation, and the sword of the Spirit, which is the word of God," *Verse 18*. "Praying always with all prayer and supplication in the spirit, and watching there unto with all perseverance and supplication for all saints." Then, and only then, will you be ready to take the battlefield against the devil and his army.

Those brave and honorable souls who faithfully attend the tens of thousands of black churches across the length and breath of these United States, and who long to see God move and His power made manifest, must first, trust Him enough to stand up and step out on His word. There must first be an act of faith demonstrated by challenging fraud religions that are currently being perpetrated on the masses of poor hopeless black people by the established black church leadership. Furthermore, there must not merely be a blanket rejection of the distorted version of the gospel that is currently being taught in the great majority of our black churches by the current crop of misguided leadership, but a simultaneous production of truth obtained from diligent study and rational analysis of the scriptures. In that way one can ascertain the true role of the black man in the legitimate Bible. As I have already stated with the emphasis of reason and the sanctity of conviction, that the only true and authentic version of the Bible period, is the black man's story. It is a historical fact that Jesus Christ lived on this earth in the flesh as a black African man. Furthermore, nearly every single character in the scriptures, if the truth was ever told, was actually an African. We must also resolve to research the scriptures through the eyes and mind of the Holy Spirit in order that we may truly find the knowledge of God, and finally see the wisdom of His divine purpose and will for His people. Moreover, we must be honest enough to ask God to deliver us from our own deep-seated psychological affliction of ethnic inferiority so that we can accept His divine and eternal truth when He reveals it to us, even if that truth issues from the lips of a black man. Also, we must pray that Jesus will finally lift the veil of centuries of racist dogma that has so thoroughly white washed our minds and blinded us, so that we can finally honestly and truthfully bring ourselves to respect and accept the volumes of rigorously scientific and methodologically sound biblical research done by Africans and African Americans, as legitimate and valid scholarship.

I submit that through the sincere study and research of the scriptures, combined with a sincere relationship with God the Father, He will reveal to us His divine and eternal truth. This is the only valid interpretation of the scriptures. From this new inter-

pretation, we will finally assume our proper relationship with God and at last take our rightful psychological, economic, and political place among the rest of
the family of man. Then we shall be truly spiritually
energized to organize, mobilize, and implement
social and economic programs to uplift our people in
the same way that other ethnic groups have done for
generations here in America.

CHAPTER 9

The Feminization of the Black Church

If one was to observe the congregational composition of the great majority of African-American churches throughout this nation, the evidence would reveal that they are overwhelmingly female. Why is this the case? What does this really mean? What are the real implications of this situation with regards to the prospect of black family stability and cohesion? I submit, that when one takes an honest look at this situation and endeavors to undertake a rational analysis of it, the conclusions yielded by such an analysis will be ominous and far more disturbing than things appear on the surface.

First of all, I contend that the African-American church is overwhelmingly female because of the nature of its message. In other words, its version of the gospel is so feminized and bereft of any real power and influence over the lives of its parishioners, that it is viewed as basically irrelevant to the daily lives of most black men. The miserable failure of the black church to seriously address those basic bread and butter issues like jobs, education, housing, crime, and healthcare has made it irrelevant and obsolete in the eyes of most black men. Moreover, even its wholesale abandonment of those moral values like the sanctity of marriage and family, respect, responsibility, and economic accountability has made the black church appear too effeminate, soft, and week to inspire the allegiance of most black men. This is why most of the black churches are filled, for the most part, with women and children.

For some reason, black women seem to have a greater emotional need than black men to belong to, and be a part of a social institution like the church. Their attachment to the church apparently gives them some sense of belonging and purpose. Therefore, church affiliation is one of the socially acceptable ways that women can satisfy this psychological need. I suppose this deep emotional need stems from the unavailability of suitable black men for marriage and family life. However, I submit that this phenomenon can be attributed to the predominance of a spineless, heartless, and lily-livered clergy which insists on avoiding those basic social, economic, and moral issues which most black men are concerned about, and are essential to the survival of black folk in this nation.

Most black men, especially those who have been, or are still apart of the street life, can readily understand and appreciate a hustle or a scam when they see one. This is why most of them have totally rejected the black preacher and the black church establishment. They have known for years what is really going on in most of our black churches. They also know that many of the black preachers acquired their skills as hustlers and scam artists in the streets. Sadly, too many of these so-called preachers have never really changed their hustling ways. They have simply moved to another venue to ply their trade. As a result, many a street-wise black man can realize and appreciate the fact that one hustler can definitely recognize another. Many of these pastors are so brazen that they continue to lead their clandestine street lives while simultaneously playing the holy role in the church. In other words, many of them continue to use illicit drugs, gamble, chase women, and engage in all types of vice and sin. Nevertheless, they continue to stand behind the sacred desk and piously proclaim to their congregations that they have been called and anointed by god to lead them. This kind of pathetic hypocrisy has made many black preachers objects of the vilest contempt in the eyes of those men who know them, for who and what they really are. As a result, many black preachers are viewed by most street-wise black men as playing the same games as hustlers play in the streets, and they are held in the vilest contempt and rankest disdain, because they have stooped to doing their dirt under the guise of religion. The great majority of black men resent the church for its ruthless exploitation of their sisters, wives, daughters, aunts, mothers and grandmothers. They stand back and watch their women give their money and literally their whole lives to the church, and then when they become old and sick and need help themselves, the church invariably turns its sanctimonious back on them. This is the bitter disgust and boiling anger that I have heard so many black men express about the black church over the years. They feel, and I think rightly so, that the black church is little more than a thinly disguised racket designed to support and sustain a greedy, hypocritical, and hopelessly self-indulgent clergy class.

As a result, most sober minded and critically thinking black men view the church with disdain, disgust, and deep suspicion. What tangible projects or programs to really benefit the average parishioner can these church leaders point to as a constructive use of the millions of dollars that they take in year after year? What legitimate examples can they point to as concrete evidence of any economic development that they have undertaken in the black community? Where is the discussion of even considering an agenda for economic development and self-determination for the black community? These are the primary reasons why most black men stay away from the black church. They feel that it is little more than a sophisticated street hustle, designed to use, abuse, and exploit their women in the name of Christianity.

However, it seems as if most black women have not been as critical in their thinking, with regard to the true motives of the black clergy. I feel that this may be a result of a variety of factors. For example, the critical shortage of available black men for marriage and family life, in light of the over arching need of many black women to be a part of what they perceive as a wholesome social organization, could be one factor for women's unwavering support of the church. Another may be due to the fact that most black females seem to have a much stronger tradition of "church affiliation" than most black men have had over the years. Also, in the absence of a strong, wholesome, committed relationship with a black man, and an unmet need for emotional fulfillment, they see their Jesus and religion as a way to fill this critical void in their lives.

Unfortunately, this does not, in most cases, satisfy that physical and emotional need for male contact. Consequently, many of these women are yet forced to deal with men who have no interest or desire to become a part of the church. On the contrary, these men, especially if they are from the streets, are usually very hostile toward the church and will often try to pull these women away from it. As a result, these women often find themselves in a hopeless tug of war as they desperately try to hold on to both, the men they love and the church too. Tragically, these kinds of relationships are almost always doomed to failure and what is even more tragic, is that they often produce children. Consequently, the children produced from these transitory relationships are doomed to grow up in poverty, or at best in a single female-headed household. Unfortunately, this constant battle between the psychological and the physical and the emotional and the spiritual, is a reality for most young women, especially those of child- bearing age, in many a black church congregation.

This phenomenon of filling the black church with women and children actually does absolutely nothing as far as promoting any credible example of the sanctity of marriage and the value of family cohesion in the black community. Unless or until the black church leadership is forced to deal with the actual bread and butter issues crucial to African-American survival in this country, the black church will remain far more a part of the problem in the community than any part of a real solution. Most black men will remain hostile toward the church as long as they feel that it is siphoning money away from them through their women. This makes them feel that the church is doing nothing but further exploiting them through their women for the benefit of a heartless and insatiably greedy clergy. They see this clergy as a class of parasitic leaches that gives them nothing in return but pompous pretension and a gilded gospel that is ineffective and obsolete. The complaints are legion from black men who have seen their women give their money, and literally their whole lives to the church, but the very moment that they needed something, the church wasn't there for them. Many of these women, after giving the best years of their lives in loyal and dedicated service to the church, are resigned to spend their twilight years in nursing homes, abandoned and alone. The church has abandoned them when they needed it most. I have known many women personally, who have worked diligently in the church for all their adult lives only to find that when they grew old and in poor health, their so called church family turned its sanctimonious back on them. My God! What about the scriptural charge to the church concerning taking care of the widows and the orphans? I submit that the only charge that the great majority of the black clergy have embraced in any shape, form, or fashion, is that of taking care of its greedy and pathetically pompous self, and it has done that superbly. Many black men cannot bring themselves to respect or trust the black clergy because they can't see anything redeeming in its behavior that represents positive and constructive activity in the community.

In his secret heart, the average black man deeply resents the black clergy for its influence over, and exploitation of, his woman. Furthermore, he sees the preacher as a rival for the affection and admiration of his woman. Moreover, he often sees the preacher, operating under the guise of pastor and spiritual leader, as the major competitor for influence over his woman. He resents deeply the fact that she is often far more motivated to cook, clean, sew, and do all manner of domestic tasks under the guise of "church work", for the preacher, than she ever seems to be willing to do for him in the home. She is often far more apt to listen to, and accept the advice of the preacher, than she is willing to accept from him. She seems willing to work harder, longer, and with more zeal for the preacher than she does for him. Moreover, her liberality with the purse strings is more often than not, more in the preacher's favor, than in the husband's. As a result, the black man becomes hostile and even bitter because he feels that he is not the primary object of his woman's affection, or the chief authority in his own household. Consequently, compared to the preacher, he feels diminished and insignificant in his woman's eyes. Therefore, he inevitably responds with hostility and resentment toward her.

As a result, the sycophantic loyalty, and unctuous affection, on the part of far too many black women for their pastors becomes the primary source of hostility and resentment in their relationship with their men. I have actually heard many a black man say with bitter disgust and derision, "My wife acts more like she's married to the preacher than she does to me." This is that bitterness and resentment which courses just beneath the surface placidity like a dangerous under current in many a relationship between black men and women who are involved in the church. So, it is this kind of built-in volatility, and resulting fragility in so many black male/female relationships which accounts for the fact that so many black churches are filled with nothing but widowed, divorced, separated, and single women and their children. I submit that the current black clergy is so out of step and out of touch with the larger community, that it doesn't know, or simply doesn't care about the true spiritual, moral, or economic health of the black family. If it were, there would be honest Christian teaching taking place with regard to just how Christian men and women are supposed to behave in a marital relationship. A woman is supposed to submit herself to her own husband, not the preacher! A true Christian woman is commanded by god, to love, honor and ultimately obey the will of her own husband, not the preacher! The scripture commands that a true Christian man is to submit himself to the divine will of God and love his wife as Christ loves the church. *I Cor. 11: 3-16*. A true Christian man is more than willing to love, honor, cherish, and most of all protect and provide for his wife. He is willing to give his life for her, just as Jesus Christ was willing to give his life for the church. *Eph. 5: 22-33. Col. 3: 18-19. 1st. Tim. 2: 11-14. 1st Peter. 3: 1-7*. So, what is the true and proper role of the wife in a Christian marriage? What is the true role and responsibility of a husband? What is the true role of a pastor in his position as a spiritual leader of a Christian family? Until and unless these fundamental questions are honestly researched and then forthrightly addressed in the fullness of their natural and spiritual implications

136

according to the divine will of God, there will be no positive change in the black church nor will there be any constructive impact on the black family.

The black clergy cannot be trusted to honestly address these essential and most fundamental questions of marriage and family. Why? Because it has not done so in any serious way up to this point. Therefore, it is doubtful that it ever will address these profound and fundamental questions in any significant way. They won't, because most of these black preachers can offer their congregations no credible examples of stable, loving, Christian families themselves. Hence, they are more than satisfied with things just the way that they are. They are more than content with the prospect that they have no critically thinking, progressive-minded, socially conscious young black men in their congregations who might challenge their reactionary philosophy of Christianity and ineffective leadership. These misguided keepers of the status quo, are too deaf, dumb, blind, and spiritually dead themselves, to realize the role that they're playing in the disintegration of the black family. On the other hand, maybe they do know, and just simply do not care about the tragic impact of their own villainy.

As I have said so many times throughout this book, this kind of moral, ethical, and spiritual honesty will not and cannot be expected to come from the culprits who are responsible for such utter chaos and colossal social disorganization now so pervasive in the black community. Those men and women who have established a relationship with the God of the universe and are led by His Holy spirit to address this rampant sin, will have to step forward. Any truthful and honest study of the non-Western European version of Christianity will lead one to the conclusion that it is a spiritually galvanizing, and morally activating force in one's life. It is not a spectator sport. All must get into the fray. Paul said, that we must put on the whole armor because we are in a spiritual war. Those who are not standing up against sin and wickedness are just as guilty as those who are actually engaging in, or promoting it. This is not a war that allows any one to be neutral on any issue. True Christians are commanded to love that which God loves, and hate that which God hates, and there is simply no middle ground.

Therefore, the true Christian must stand up and speak out against that which is morally, ethically, and spiritually wrong and stand up for that which is morally, ethically, and spiritually right according to the unadulterated word of God. This means that there will be great opposition to any real change because most of the black clergy is perfectly satisfied with things just the way that they are. So it would be a total waste of time to expect any genuine move toward positive change from this group. This kind of honest and sincere search for truth and then the application of that truth simply will not, and cannot come from the current spiritually dead, intellectually pathetic, and morally impotent church leadership. This action will ultimately have to come from the few faithful who actually have a heart for receiving the truth of god, and a mind for doing His divine will on this earth.

Unfortunately, the great majority of the black clergy and parishioners alike, who so piously declare to the world that they are saved, sanctified, filled with the Holy ghost, and living righteously, are actual examples of none of these things. All one has to do is observe the glaring discrepancy between their profession of Holiness and the scandalous sinfulness of their behavior. So this kind of spirituality and Holiness that these hypocrites so piously proclaim to the world that they indeed possess, can only be made manifest in one's life as a result of a true and intimate relationship with God. Furthermore, the kind of love that will compel one to stand up for truth, justice, and righteousness without fear in the face of so much opposition can only come from the indwelling of the Holy spirit of God in one's heart and soul. Consequently, this is not a battle for hypocrites, the faint-hearted, or those who are just playing at being Christians, because the stakes are just too high and the price is just too exacting.

The black church must be forced to teach men and women, by spiritual precept and living example, how to truly love and respect one another. It must teach the values of family, unity, love of self, responsibility, and most of all, accountability to God and one's fellowmen. The church is supposed to represent on this earth, a perfect example of the family, with Jesus Christ as the head and all true believers as the body. Consequently, the human family is supposed to be replicated in the exact image of the church. The man is supposed to be the high priest of his household and accorded the respect, love, and honor commensurate with that position. *I Cor. 7: 2-16. I Cor. 11: 3*. Also, it is axiomatic, that he is supposed to be responsible for providing love, material and emotional support, and security for his family. The wife is supposed to be submissive to her husband as a Christian unto God. She is supposed to be a source of love and support to her husband and children. *Proverbs. 22: 6. Eph. 6: 2. Exo. 20: 12.* The black church must also be willing to embark upon a rigorous and critical analysis of the negative psychological impact that North American slavery has had on the collective psyche of African-Americans.

Furthermore, it has to understand and come to grips with the protracted problems perpetuated by the body of extremely negative values, of innate inferiority and deep-seated beliefs of self-hatred that have been embraced and internalized by African-Americans. This psychologically dysfunctional taint is still being transmitted from one generation to the next through American educational and social institutions. The church must be willing to analyze and try to understand the matrix of Western Culture and how it has dehumanized, despised, reviled, and rejected the black man and everything African. Therefore, the imposition of centuries of these tremendously negative cultural beliefs, values, and self-destructive behavior patterns, embraced and internalized by generations of black people, have contributed to the profound lack of trust, love, and respect between black men and women.

These debilitating maladies continue to severely militate against the establishment of healthy and mutually respectful relationships between black men and women. Only the creation of such healthy relationships between black men and women will foster respect, true love, affection, and cooperation which are essential for the maintenance of a stable and wholesome family. For example, the slave masters have used strong black men for generations as studs to sire babies in order to increase the economic value of their human property. However, these slave studs have never had the legal and moral responsibility for raising and providing for their offspring imposed upon them. Similarly, black women have been used for centuries as breeders. However, they have not been socially conditioned in the same way as other women, to expect their men to provide for them and their offspring. Conversely, because of the plantation culture and their slave indoctrination, they were taught to ascribe that responsibility to their slave masters. This social pathology has not disappeared, because in recent years, black women have assigned this responsibility to the government. Therefore, there must be an honest admission on the part of black men and women of their complicity and culpability in creating and then maintaining the sorry social condition of the black community. Both sexes have been so systematically and diabolically used by slave masters and as a result, both sexes have embraced and internalized these most negative values and have maintained the unhealthy predilection to persist in these destructive patterns of behavior. However, the black man has to confess that he is the chief culprit responsible for the sorry state of his own community.

Why? Because he is the natural, as well as the divinely ordained, head of the family. Moreover, he is

141

the head of his community. Yet, because of his irresponsible sex and production of legions of children that he cannot, or will not, provide for, they are doomed to grow up in neglect and poverty. These are the children who grow up to duplicate the same negative, self-destructive patterns of behavior as their parents. This has resulted in the present explosion of single female-headed households and pervasive neglect and grinding poverty which is the face of the urban centers across this nation. Then there is the unmitigated fact that the black man has been historically stripped of nearly every legitimate opportunity to establish an economic power base for himself in this nation. The establishment of such an economic base could have given him some measure of freedom and independence from the total domination by the white power elite. Since the arrival of the black African on these shores, his very survival has depended upon the caprice or whimsicality of white people. As a result, his woman has been forced to operate in the role as head of the family by raising the children much of the time, without his help, protection, or support. She has been indoctrinated by this racist culture to regard the black man as trifling, trivial, and insignificant. Moreover, with the advent of her access to a myriad of social welfare programs, and of late, far greater employment opportunities, she has actually been convinced that she can get along just fine without him.

Therefore, she neither admires nor respects him as a real man; nor can she bring herself to submit to the black man in any natural or spiritual way that women of other ethnic groups can submit to their men. She has not been socialized to believe that the black man isn't intrinsically fit to be regarded as a high priest in the home, nor is he worthy to hold a position of authority over her. Therefore, she cannot find it within her heart and soul to submit to him, hold him in esteem, or obey him regardless of what she may have promised to do in a marriage contract. These are the kinds of critical and extremely destructive social dynamics of culture and socialization that have been imposed on black folk in America for generations. These powerful and extremely destructive negative values all but guarantee that black men and women will find it virtually impossible to truly love, respect, trust, honor, or cooperate with each other in any meaningful way.

Consequently, there must be spiritually serious and scientifically rigorous investigation into this extremely negative cultural indoctrination of blacks. We must endeavor to understand and change these extremely destructive social and cultural dynamics which have been imposed on black men and women since our arrival on these shores. Unfortunately, this kind of consciousness raising, scientifically rigorous, and spiritually sound teaching is totally absent in the great majority of black churches. There is virtually no real in-depth, honest, and systematic teaching on the sanctity of marriage, the importance of family, and the proper behavior of husband, wife, and children in a Christian marriage taking place in most black churches. Consequently, the results of such a tragic omission are painfully obvious throughout our community. There are as many divorces taking place among black folk who are supposed to be Christians these days as there are among those who never professed to know Jesus Christ at all. Also, the incidence of illegitimate births is just as rampant in black churches as they are in the general society. Furthermore, there is so little difference between the so called, "Christian life style " and non Christians in most aspects of life in this nation, that one is hard pressed to see any substantial difference between the two. Consequently, this sad observation accounts for the fact that there is little respect, and even less reverence accorded to the black church, and to the church in general in America.

If the black church is ever going to be a true representative of god's perfect family, it must first line up to God's perfect will. I submit that this can only be accomplished by a true repentance for sin, and the sincere acceptance of Jesus Christ as Lord and Savior. Most so called, "Christians", are willing to spout off in their pseudo-holy bombast, "I am saved, and I know that I'm saved. I'm saved, sanctified, and filled with the Holy Ghost!"

However, the acid test of all these boastful claims is the manifestation of spiritual fruit in the individual's life, or lack thereof. When a person proclaims that he or she is saved and Jesus Christ is the Lord of his or her life, it is supposed to mean the individual is actually willing to live for Him. However, herein lies the problem with the great majority of so called Christians. Most people who claim to be Christians, preachers and parishioners alike, in their secret hearts, simply have no genuine desire to live for Jesus Christ. They only desire to live for themselves. Therefore, under the guise of Christianity, that is actually what they do.

This is why the black church is little more than a social organization that most people join for the purpose of emotional fulfillment. It is fashionable to attend church these days, and the great majority of so called Christians attend church for reasons that have absolutely nothing at all to do with Jesus Christ or living Holy. One needs only to observe their scurrilous and scandalous behavior which is anything but Christian. They simply want and need something to belong to, and feel that they are a part of. However, going to church can no more actually make you a Christian than going to a garage can make you a mechanic. There has to be a deeper spiritual transformation that can only be achieved by the actual submission of one's life and will to God's. However, the great majority of us are simply not willing to do this. Yes, we say to the world, and each other, that we have submitted our lives to God, but we know in our secret heart of hearts, that we are lying. Furthermore, the evidence of our dishonesty ultimately reflects itself in our attitudes and behavior. We claim with our mouths that we love God and that Jesus Christ is the Lord of our lives. Yet, we consistently do the most Ungodly things to one another and ourselves. We say that we love the truth, but we refuse to actually embrace that truth, especially when it demands that we relinquish our own selfish, and self-centered motivations, in favor of a God centered life that true Christian love requires of us. We sanctimoniously proclaim to each other, and the whole world, that we've been born again, and that we are saved, sanctified, and filled with the Holy Ghost. Yet, our behavior says unmistakably, that we in fact are none of these things. Most of us avow Christ with our mouths, but our hearts are far from Him. It is this kind of wholesale dishonesty in the Christian church in general, and in the black church in particular, that makes the western European brand of Christianity, appear as little more than a sham, a fraud, and a cruel joke.

There can't possibly be any vertical connection with god without the horizontal expression of His spirit in one's social relationships. In other words, the only true spirituality that one actually possesses in his heart is that which he expresses in his daily life through the interaction with others. It is shamefully hypocritical for the clergy to talk about the church body as being the spiritual family of God, and then make absolutely no sincere effort to teach men and women how to be examples of a physical family here on this earth. It is sheer mockery for preachers to preach to the black man that he must be the head of his own household and then turn around and emasculate him in the eyes of his wife and children. Preachers do this by making black women feel that they should be more loyal to the preacher and the church than to the husband and father in the home. Furthermore, it is simply insane to tell the black man that he must provide for and support his family while the church simply stands on the sideline in sanctimonious piety raking in millions of dollars but staunchly refusing to even attempt to create job opportunities for him.

This is why most black men have such deep-seated contempt and resentment for the black church because it has become quite vociferous in pointing out his failings in its unrelenting criticism of him, but has yet to step forward to do something economically, in any concrete way, to help him. As a result, the church merely continues to be for most black men, just another obstacle to their development and a further drain on the already meager resources of their households. Therefore, many a black man cannot bring himself to respect the black preacher, or respond in the affirmative to his silver tongued requests to come into the fold. He sees him as just another slick hustler running a scandalous game. Consequently, this is why most black men will not become involved in the black church, because they can't see anything tangible that it is doing in the community. They see it as too controlling of their women, to intrusive in their homes, and too exploitative of their families.

If the black man in America is ever going to become a serious component of the Christian church, the church will have to honestly and sincerely address itself to those issues and values basic to his survival. Again, it must embrace those issues like jobs, education, health care, housing, crime, and those values such as self-respect, honesty, family cohesion, marriage, and responsibility. These issues and values are crucial to the very survival of the black man in this nation. Therefore, the extent to which these issues and values are seriously addressed by the black clergy will determine whether black men will ever change their overwhelmingly negative view of the black church.

Therefore, its incumbent upon those few honest and sincere black men now in the church, who understand and realize the fact that the church must address the material as well as the spiritual needs of the black man. Those who have the love of God in them, to act in a constructive way and tackle those "bread and butter" issues will be the salvation of the black community. However, the focus on these critical issues and crucial values are currently so pitifully lacking in most black churches, that black men feel they are totally justified in staying away. The job of addressing these issues and values will have to be done by those who clearly understand that the black family can never hope to be saved until, or unless, the black man is saved. How can any family survive and thrive, and realize its fullest potential without its natural and divinely ordained head? So, it's time for action by those few black men who are already in the church and who have actually accepted Jesus Christ as their Lord and Savior. For only they who know the truth and have embraced that truth can reach those who are still seeking truth. I truly believe that black men would come in to the church in masse, if they could be sincerely convinced that the church is committed to doing that which is naturally right and spiritually righteous. If they could be shown by a radical change in its behavior, that would prove to them that the church was really about God's business instead of pontificating its empty bombast and self-deluded rhetoric, perhaps they might seriously consider coming into the fold. They want to be a part of a church that respects them as men and is willing to address their spiritual and material needs. They don't need the church to merely tell them how they have failed as men, but to teach them by spiritual precept and living example, how to be successful husbands and fathers and walk in god's love and perfect will for their lives. They are watching and waiting for the church to do something more than just talk about the love and power of Christ, they want to feel it and see it through the example of positive behavior and constructive action.

Unfortunately, the great majority of the black church leadership is so thoroughly lost itself, that it doesn't have a clue as to what the real problems confronting average black men actually are. The black man has been so thoroughly emasculated in America, that he has been forced to exist in a variable no man's land of psychological, political, economic, and especially spiritual nothingness. He has been totally castrated and rendered impotent in every significant way that really matters in the lives of other men on this planet. For example, he produces nothing, builds nothing, owns nothing, controls nothing, stands for nothing, and he is committed to nothing except his own self-destruction. He has no conscious history except for that distorted, disjointed, and thoroughly uninspiring saga provided him by the negative experience of American education. So, he plans for others, creates for others, builds for others, memorizes the histories of others, but is motivated to do absolutely nothing for himself. However, to be honest enough to admit these things is so excruciatingly painful to the black man, that he has resulted in all manner of escapism in order to perfect his absolute denial. Consequently, this painful reality is so emotionally devastating to even contemplate for the great majority of black men, that they simply cannot abide any honest analysis of their pitiful plight in America. In order to have a prayer for a chance at mental, psychological, and especially spiritual health, the black man must have enough courage to honestly face the painfully pathetic truth about himself.

The black church, top heavy with a reactionary, thoroughly uneducated, and spiritually dysfunctional clergy imposing its white washed, brain dead version of Christianity on the people will not and cannot, save the souls of black men. The black church is too busy blaming the victims for their own utterly sorry plight. These black men who cannot bring themselves into the church have already concluded that, the church, in its present impotent and morally bankrupt state, has nothing to offer them. These men are hurting and because of that hurt they have become angry. They understand all too painfully well, that they do not produce or control anything of economic significance in this country. They know that they have no power to even control the economics of their own community, and even more pathetic, the economics of their own individual households. They have been rendered dispensable by a society who rejects and reviles them as trivial and insignificant. What is far more tragic than this is the fact that this larger societal view of him has been embraced and internalized by so many black women. As a result, they have begun to relate to the black man as an insignificant and dispensable component of the black community. Therefore, his hurt and anger are further compounded, and out of his morbid fear of the white man and white society, he lashes out in pain and anger at his own woman and children. Sadly, this is the pathetic

150

reality of the black man in America. So, until or unless the black church is spiritually sincere enough, morally courageous enough, and intellectually honest enough to address this reality, nothing at all in the African-American community will change.

The primary theological training and educational orientation of the black clergy has simply not equipped black preachers to deal with the real cultural, psychological, economic, and spiritual problems impacting the black community. The great majority of black preachers received the same biblically distorted and brain dead religious education and training as white preachers receive in the various schools of divinity around this nation. As a result, their outlook and orientation to the scriptures is just as thoroughly distorted as their white counterparts when it comes to teaching and preaching the true gospel of Jesus Christ. This is why the black church, in its present state, has absolutely nothing to offer the black man. So, unless there is a fundamental change in this approach to the gospel, and a genuine concern for his soul, the black man will continue to view the church with distrust, disdain, and contempt.

Consequently, it is left up to those honest souls who have discovered the true, historically valid and spiritually legitimate Jesus Christ, and who have established an intimate relationship with Him, to carry out the true mission of the church. These are those who will be moved by Christ's love and compassion to reach out to the black man and show him through their living example, what real Christian love and true soul salvation is. It is the job of those who really know God and who have submitted themselves to His will, to lead black men out of the impenetrable darkness of their spiritual dungeon and break their psychological shackles. The shackles which continue to bind them in powerlessness, hopelessness, and ignorance and have aided in his self-hatred and self-destruction. I am referring to those few true Christians who realize that you cannot help black men by blaming them totally for their sorry state. Those who understand that in a culture where ones intrinsic worth is measured by what kind of job one has, how much money one makes, and what kind of car he or she drives, the black man will always come up short. This is because black men do not control the allocation of jobs and wealth in this society.

So, until and unless he does become a significant player in this equation, it is the grandest folly for him to subscribe to such an absurd standard for measuring self-worth. Furthermore, he must be taught once and for all, how to love and appreciate his own cultural and physical uniqueness. God made him black, gave him his broad nose, woolly hair and thick lips. Yet he has been indoctrinated to hate himself, and made to feel ashamed of his own ethnicity by a racist white culture which has sought in every conceivable way, to debase, dehumanize, and demean him. He has been systematically robbed of the true knowledge of himself. He has had that knowledge erased by a history of four hundred years of chattel slavery, and indoctrinated for countless generations with a body of racist dogma that has taught him to profoundly hate himself. However, now it is possible to reclaim much of that critical knowledge of the African self, but it can

152

only be taught in the church because it has never been, and will never be allowed to be taught in public schools. Therefore, it must be the business of the church to teach the black man the truth about himself so that he can turn away from his learned patterns of destructive behavior and begin the heeling process. For, the scripture declares that the consequence of ignorance is the greatest tragedy, and sadly, the African living in America is the very personification of such a tragedy. Hosea Chapter 4, verse 6: "My people are destroyed for lack of knowledge." The Black man is desperately ill and the Christian church should be one place where he can come and be finally healed of his psychologically and spiritually terminal illness. However, because it, by and large, is a church in name only, and stands as a pathetic example of the worst conceivable hypocrisy, it is of no spiritual, psychological, or economic value to him, or to those who sadly give their lives to support and sustain it. Therefore, it will only be through the love and power of the true and living God that black men and all men can ever be saved from their sins. So again, those who have the sincere and honest desire to seek the truth and then, commit themselves to that truth will ultimately make a difference. "Ye shall know the truth, and the truth shall make you free", *John 8:32*. Nothing short of the unadulterated truth, the truth about his own black African self, and the gospel truth, will make the black man free, and able to stand up and be all that God intended for him to be. Christ said, "If I be lifted up, I will draw all men unto me," *John 12:32*. The reason many black men, especially those who are sincere, sober-minded, and street-wise cannot bring themselves to be a part of the church, is because they see nothing there that they can honestly respect or admire, much less love or revere.

CHAPTER 10

Body, Soul, and Spirit

The basic definition of a religion is: any philosophy, doctrine, or ideology which constitutes a system of basic beliefs and values embraced by its adherent. As a result, this religious frame of reference then becomes that individual's worldview. In other words, a religion then becomes, for those who subscribe to it, the very foundation upon which they build their lives. Many African-Americans have concluded, and I agree, that white supremacy, not Christianity, is the most powerful, pervasive, and widely practiced religion in Western European Culture. So, the religion becomes the individual's primary frame of reference governing the particular adherent's behavior in all human relations. Religion provides purpose, continuity, and an inner equilibrium which helps him or her cope with the vicissitudes of life on earth, where there is often little that is constant or certain. True religion however, most of which is divinely centered, is the force in an individual's life which provides definite answers to the most basic and fundamental questions about life and death. It helps him to achieve wholeness and a real sense of inner peace that is a result of that wholeness. However, this wholeness can only be achieved when, or if, the religious doctrine is complete in its definition of human existence. In other words, whether that doctrine fully and clearly addresses each dimension of man as a living being.

Unfortunately, this is where Christianity, as it is being taught in the black church has serious problems. It has simply failed miserably to provide African-American parishioners with a holistic approach to it as a living faith. In the great majority of black churches, there is pitifully little useful teaching on the natural or material needs of the individual. The pathetic refusal to address those physical needs of the individual and even the clergy's brazen contempt at the idea of even considering such material needs, is a sorry testament to this fact. In previous pages I have already discussed the black church's all but total resistance to the notion of any form of genuine economic development in the community. Now however, I am going to talk about its dismal failure to address even those basic physical health and subsistence needs of its faithful. I have read in the Bible and heard black preachers proclaim with sanctimonious profundity, "The body is the temple of the Holy Spirit." Well now, if they really believe this, which I sincerely doubt that they do, then why don't they teach people how to properly care for their bodies? I heard the comedian Dick Gregory say once, that pork chops, ham hocks, and fried chicken have killed more black folk than the Ku Klux Klan. Although Mr. Gregory's statement had a comic ring to it, it was nonetheless, sadly true. Due to the low socio-economic status of the great majority of African-Americans, coupled with their woeful lack of information about proper diet and nutrition, it is little wonder why we lead the list in every conceivable category when it come to the incidence of diseases directly related to diet. African-Americans are two to three times more likely to die from diabetes, high blood pressure, heart

156

disease, stroke, and certain types of cancer than the rest of the population. Unfortunately, these diseases and maladies are directly related to diet. Moreover, what is even more tragic is that with the practice of good health habits and proper nutrition, these maladies can be prevented. Again, this is where the black church has failed, and failed miserably in terms of a holistic approach to the gospel.

People, especially the church faithful, should be taught proper nutrition and good health habits as stringently as they are taught about sin. In other words, the teaching of health and nutrition should be an integral part of church doctrine and given the same time and attention as the teaching on purely spiritual matters. Most other religions have as a basic component of their doctrines, specific instructions with regards to guidelines for proper health and nutrition. What earthly good is a man or woman if he or she is "spiritually fit" and a physical wreck as a result of practicing poor dietary habits? Eating fried, greasy, fatty foods like chicken, pork chops, fat back, and ham, coupled with heavy starchy foods like potato salad, macaroni and cheese, yams, and all manner of sugar filled desserts are sadly a tradition in the great majority of the black churches in this nation. This unhealthy preoccupation with the regular consumption of the worst types of food has taken a dev· astating toll on the physical health of black Christians. This is why the need for the teaching of health and fitness and proper diet and nutrition is so crucial in the black church. This represents a glaring failure of the black clergy to grasp and understand the tremendous neglect of the health and physical welfare of the faithful. Also, it further underscores the fact that this reactionary, self-indulgent group is not spiritually fit, intellectually capable, or morally qualified to lead the flock.

The only teaching that it seems to be genuinely concerned with is those most superficial matters of style and elegance. Most black preachers are only too anxious to teach, by living example, the art of fancy dressing and pompous pretension. This all-consuming obsession with stylish clothes, fancy cars, and flashy dressing is the quintessential desire of far too many black Christians. Unfortunately, so much emphasis has been placed on this kind of ludicrous superficiality, that many a sincere soul earnestly desiring to become a part of the church body, has been discouraged because of this all consuming obsession with fancy dressing, fashion profiling, and pompous posturing in the church. Many of those who are on fixed incomes, unemployed, or working poor, often cannot afford the expensive brand-named designer clothes which seem to be required attire for too many "church people". Those who are not so financially able are often made to feel out of place and oftentimes not welcome in their less expensive attire. They are told loudly and clearly by the condescending looks, snooty sneers, sardonic whispers, and all manner of non-verbal communication by those shallow-minded, pseudo-Christian hypocrites that they are not welcome in their petty bourgeois tabernacle. James I 1-10. This again, only poignantly underscores my contention of how hopelessly lost these so called "Christians" really are. Their common sense is so distorted and their minds have been so jaded with the

158

idea of their own self-righteousness, that they cannot even perceive just how totally and pathetically wrong they really are.

The whole message of the true gospel of Jesus Christ is focused on the salvation of the unseen, the supernatural, the immortal soul, and the inner man, not the flesh. John 4:24. "God is a Spirit; and they that worship him must worship in spirit and truth." John 3:16. "For God so loved the world, that he gave his only begotten son, and who so ever believeth in him shall not perish, but have eternal life." John 3:1-; verse 5: Jesus answered, "Verily, Verily, I say unto thee, except a man be born of water and of the Spirit, he cannot enter into the kingdom of God." Ezekiel 18:4: "Behold, all souls are mine; as the soul of the father, so also the soul of the son is mine; the soul that sinneth, it shall die." Yet in light of the obvious and primary concern of Jesus Christ with the soul, these gaudy hypocrites are obsessed with style, form, fashion, and flesh. These are the most grotesque, superficial, and transitory components of human existence. It is this kind of perverse and pathetically superficial trifling with the gospel, that has made the black church everything, but what God intended. This is why it has no power, no love, and no redeeming grace for the true salvation of souls. The Black Church's narrow-minded and myopic focus on the flesh, what little attention there is concerning the health and fitness of the natural body, is totally that of vanity and narcissism. It is not interested in teaching men and women about diet and proper health practices which could no doubt result in longer and healthier lives, but the primary focus is that of conspicuous consumption and gaudy ostentation. If there were half as much time and attention given to the teaching of proper health and nutrition in the black church as there is dedicated to the superficiality of style and dress, there would be a far healthier church. As a result, it would be a far more productive church.

Yes, the body is the temple of the Holy Spirit. This is why it must be seriously understood, and properly cared for. I Corinthians 6:19-20: "What! Know ye not that your body is the temple of the Holy Ghost which is in you, which ye have of God, and ye are not your own!" Verse 20: "For ye are bought with a price; therefore glorify God in your body, and in your spirit, which are God's." Therefore, the unrestricted consumption of high fat, high salt, high starch and sugar-laden foods must be stopped at all cost. Furthermore, proper diet and physical fitness must be as much a part of church teaching as the teaching of the scriptures. Any preacher who claims to be called by God to lead His people and cannot see the dire need for this kind of teaching, is a liar and the truth is not in him. Whosoever God calls, He qualifies, and I submit that the great majority of the black preachers currently standing behind the sacred desk, calling themselves pastors, are neither called nor qualified to shepherd God's people. John 21:15-17: "Peter, loveth thou me, then feed my sheep." Why? Because one needs only to observe the fruit of their labor. This is the evidence that condemns them as, hopelessly lost sinners who are the most in need of salvation themselves.

Therefore, the kind of holistic Christian teaching so desperately needed in the black church will not come from a clergy which is itself in need of deliverance from its own sin and ignorance. Consequently, it will have to come from those who are really in touch with God and in tune with His will for His people. The church is the place where folk could, and should be taught the benefits of good health habits and proper nutrition. It could also teach the true meaning of the scripture that says, "Above all things, I would that you prosper and be in good health." III John verse 2: "Lo, I wish above all things that thou mayest prosper and be in health, even as thy soul prospereth." This is the kind of premium that Jesus Christ, Himself, placed on good health.

The church could, and should be the place where people could be instructed in the economic benefits of group buying. It could establish food clubs, and co-ops that would enable the people to maximize their purchasing power and minimize their individual cost. Other religious groups, social and political organizations, and groups of merchants have long used this economic strategy of group buying. Consequently, it has yielded enormous benefits for them. Moreover, this idea of food co-ops can be broadened and extended to cover other areas of durable and perishable goods. However, these kinds of extremely beneficial group purchasing strategies would require serious research and thoughtful planning on the part of church leadership. Consequently, I sincerely doubt whether the vast majority of the current black church leadership is up to the task. I am thoroughly convinced that they are too lazy, too reactionary, too complacent, too unimaginative, and irretrievably lost.

As a result of this dismal condition, this kind of innovative and constructive approach to teaching people how to adequately provide for their physical needs will have to be undertaken by those few faithful who are spiritual enough to see the dire need and have enough faith to address that need. These are the ones who will have to step forward and teach the faithful about the benefits of eating healthier, exercising more, and avoiding those foods that lead to poor health and a short life span. They must inspire in people a genuine love for fresh vegetables, fruit, fruit juices, grain products, baked fish, baked chicken, turkey and other meats low in fat, but high in protein. There is a wealth of information available on proper nutrition and how to achieve physical fitness. It is a shame, before God, that so many people believe that it is not necessary to teach it in church.

Also, there is much scientifically sound information available about drugs and alcohol, but this valuable information is viewed as being not applicable to the business of the church. It is just as much folly to believe that everyone who calls himself, or herself a Christian is true and faithful to Jesus Christ, as it is to believe that a man who contends that he has never told a lie, is telling the truth. As I have stated before, "Going to church doesn't mean that you are a true Christian any more than going into a garage means that you are a mechanic." So it is the grandest delusion to confuse church affiliation with true Christian salvation. This is why information about drugs and alcohol and sexuality should be addressed in the church and not left totally up to the public schools. At least in church, the moral and spiritual values can be integrated into the discussion. It isn't enough to tell our children to, "Just say no." to illicit sex, drugs, and alcohol. We must explain to them why they should say, "No". Then we must help them understand, by our living example, that they can only say no to drugs, alcohol, and sexual promiscuity, when they truly say yes to Jesus Christ.

It is only through the Holy Spirit of God living within the soul, that one can have the power to abstain from this kind of physically and morally destructive behavior. John 8:34-36: "Verily, Verily, I say unto you, he who committeth sin is the servant of sin, he who the son has set free, ye shall be free indeed." However, a church leadership tainted with this very sin itself, and hopelessly lost in distorted religious dogma is not qualified to teach either, by spiritual precept or living example, that which they have never truly understood or actually transcended. Therefore, only those who have received the power from God, to overcome, and whom he has ordained and anointed to teach His people can fulfill such a Holy charge. It is only those chosen few who by living example, and spiritual precept, can teach people how to overcome sin. In the final analysis, hypocrites can only teach hypocrisy, the ignorant can only teach ignorance, and fools can only teach foolishness. Therefore, only those who have been truly liberated from such things through their honest acceptance of, and obedience to the divine will of Jesus Christ can teach liberation to others. This is why the few faithful

163

who know Him and are about doing their Father's business are equipped, qualified and anointed by God to teach this divine truth.

Another component of the triumvirate of man where the black church is woefully lacking is that of the soul. Although it has given a great deal of lip service to the concept of the immortal soul, much of this information, in terms of its genuine spiritual effect, has been undermined and contradicted by the church's obsession with the physical superficiality of dress, style and elegance. As a result, this stubborn preoccupation with such transitory matters as style and appearance has, in effect, subverted the true mission of the gospel of Jesus Christ, which is the transformation of the soul through an honest and intimate relationship with Him. *Genesis 2:7*: "The Lord God formed man of the dust of the ground, and breathed into his nostrils the breath of life; and man became a living soul." The soul or spirit is the part of man that only God can observe. Therefore, it is by the true motivations and machinations of the soul that men and women are ultimately judged on that great day of God's final judgment. Consequently, the spiritual or unseen dimension of human existence is the only true reality. The soul, heart, and mind are the invisible forces that make up the essence of the man or woman that lives inside the physical body. It is that part of the human being that we can never observe with the naked eye. As long as one soul is living in the fleshly body or physical house, it can never truly observe the total essence of another soul. This ability to look upon the unmasked totality of the immortal soul is the exclusive prerogative of God.

This is why only He and He alone is qualified to make the ultimate judgment of life or death concerning the souls of men and women. Because he is omniscient, he knows every thought, deed, and motivation behind every action taken or contemplated by every living soul. This is why only he can declare that the wages of sin is death, but the gift of God is eternal life.

So only God, in all of his majesty and omniscience has the power to execute such an awesome judgment. *Romans 6:23.* It is the soul, that which is unseen, which activates that which is visible to us. It is the soul of a man or woman that activates the tongue in the articulation of speech, and is also the captain of every emotion, thought, and action. Hence the soul is the seat of all thoughts, passions, and appetites. It is in the mind or soul where all thoughts, dreams, plans, plots and schemes for good or evil are born. It is also the motivation for all overt human behavior. This is why the scriptures declare in *Proverbs 23:7*: "For as he thinketh in his heart, so is he: Eat and drink, saith he to thee; but his heart is not with thee." This is the message that Jesus brought to the people in the Sermon on the Mount. He explained to them that evil or sin is first committed in the mind or heart before it is ever acted out in overt behavior. Therefore, one is just as guilty for his or her evil thoughts as if he had actually committed the act. The soul is what Jesus Christ is concerned with because it contains the essence of the individual, the intellect, the will, and the passions or emotions. It is the complete and eternal stuff of man. So, it is the soul or mind of man that controls the body and its physical behavior. Once the soul has departed from the body, the body becomes

165

inanimate and begins to rapidly decay. We call this condition death, and when that occurs, we commit the lifeless body back to the earth from whence it originally came. Yet, while the flesh lives, it does the bidding of the soul in acts that we can observe. However, we can only assume and conjecture as to one's true intentions as a result of overt acts that we can observe.   This is why God said that we judge the tree by the fruit that it bears. In other words, we can only determine if a man or woman is actually who and what he or she claims to be, by observing his or her behavior. However, sometimes even are most careful deductions and conclusions with regard to motivations are sometimes less than accurate. We can only make deductions and draw inferences based on that which we have actually observed.

This is why god reserves the right to make the ultimate judgment of life or death. Only God has the power to observe the nakedness of an individual's soul. With our limited powers of observation and deduction, we are often times mistaken as to the true motivations of one's soul. Some people are so skilled at deception and duplicity, that they can conceal their true secret motivations and machinations. The scripture asserts that in the last days, these wolves in sheep clothing may possibly fool the very elect of God. *Matthew 24:24*: "For there shall arise false Christ's, and false prophets, and shall show great signs and wonders in so much that, if it were possible, they shall deceive the very elect." So, it is only by, and through the Holy Spirit of Christ living in us, that we can know if he is present in others. Only the Holy Spirit of Christ living within us can reveal the true unmasked characters, or souls, or hearts of others. This is called the gift of discernment, but it is only given to those who have established and maintained that intimate relationship with God. All flesh is corruptible and transitory, but the Holy Spirit of Jesus Christ is incorruptible and eternal. The world is obsessed with the physical component of human existence. People spend billions of dollars every year in fad diets and cosmetics in a vain attempt to appear youthful and sexually appealing. Many people make the most profound decisions like whom to date, whom to marry, and whom to procreate with, based almost totally on, something as superficial and transitory as, sex appeal, money, and material possessions. Although, most of us may be obsessed with the physical and material dimension of man, it is the immortal soul or spiritual dimension that concerns God. These are man's will, intellect, passions or emotions and essentially that part of him commonly referred to as the mind. It is what the Christian doctrine refers to as the inner man or the heart.

The soul or mind of man receives and perceives all information about the physical world through the five senses. However, it is only through faith and an intimate relationship with Jesus Christ, that the mind or soul, while present in the fleshly body, can experience the supernatural world. Moreover the application of this faith in order to perceive or experience the supernatural or spiritual world, works In the exact opposite way from the way things work in the physical world. For example, science and logic demand evidence. Only then is validity established. On the other hand, spirituality requires faith that a thing is, then and only then, there is evidence. "Faith is the evidence of things hoped for, and the substance of things unseen." *Hebrews 11:1*. Although, it is through the mediums of hearing, tasting, touching, seeing, and smelling that we receive all of our information about the material world. Then it is the quality of this information, combined with the consciousness of God, and an intimate relationship with him, or lack thereof, which will ultimately determine how we will interact with other human beings. As a result, the way in which the five-sense concept and spiritual information are processed by the soul, will ultimately determine whether an individual's point of view will be shaped in the image of God, or Satan.

The Bible declares that the three sinful character traits that separate man from God are, the lust of the flesh, the lust of the eye, and the pride of life. *I, John 2:15-17*. It also contends that man in his natural state; his unregenerate state is hopelessly wicked, and totally selfish. David declares in *Psalms 51:5-7*, that he was born in sin and shaped in inequity, and bereft of any good and is without repentance and acceptance of the spiritually redeeming and divine cleansing power of his creator. The scripture clearly states that the soul, who commits sin, will die. It goes on to say that he who accepts Jesus Christ as his Lord and Savior shall have eternal life in heaven with Him, *Ezekiel 18:4, John 3:16*. However, when one accepts Jesus Christ as Lord and Savior, it requires that one must then totally submit to his divine will. As I have stated before, most people who call themselves, "Christians", have no problem accepting Jesus Christ as their Savior. They cannot, however, bring themselves to accept him as their Lord.

Accepting Jesus Christ as one's Lord requires that one must then truly make him Lord, or supreme authority over his or her life. This can only be accomplished when people have totally surrendered themselves to him. In other words, when they have honestly allowed Jesus Christ's divine will to supplant their own. This is the requirement that most people who call themselves, "Christians", simply cannot, in their secret hearts abide. This is why Jesus said that in the last days there will be many who will come and say, "Lord did we not cast out demons, and do all manner of good deeds in your name; and he will say depart from me I never knew you, you workers of iniquity," *Matthew:21-23*. Because Jesus Christ is a spirit, he can actually see into the hearts and minds of all men and women. So all of the lies, shamming, and pretenses of Holiness that we declare and profess in order to fool each other does not fool him at all. Jesus Christ has the ability to look directly into the soul and observe the true character. This is the primary message that runs throughout the gospel.

Jesus Christ, is the only true example of how to live free from sin, because he totally submitted himself to the will of his Father. Consequently, he is the standard for true Christian behavior and the only criterion for a true Christian life style on this earth. The scripture states: "Let the mind of Christ, also be the mind in you," *Philippians 2:5*. "Let this mind be in you, which was also in Christ Jesus." Until and unless one has honestly repented for sin, and actually accepted Christ as Lord as well as Savior, there can be no forgiveness. It is only the Holy Spirit of Christ, living in the soul, who has the power to change an individual's perception and focus from carnality, to divinity. However, let me reiterate that one must first make Jesus Lord of his or her life. In other words, that means total submission to him, and making him the absolute authority over his or her life. Then the Holy Spirit will step in and begin the inner transformation of the soul, from an attitude of total self-centeredness to God-centeredness. Then the individual can be freed from being a slave to sin, and finally free to be a slave to Jesus Christ and his righteousness. Outside of a genuine acceptance of Jesus Christ as Lord and Savior, and a truly intimate relationship with him, through the dwelling of his Holy Spirit in one's soul, there is no possible way that anyone can delude himself into believing that he is a disciple of Jesus Christ. However, many people are actually engaged in nothing more than religious game playing and ludicrous self- deception.

The personal decision to accept Jesus Christ as one's Lord and Savior must be willful, honest, and sincere, otherwise there will be no presence of the Holy Spirit, nor can there be no real change in focus from the carnal worldly mind, to that divine mind of God's. Unfortunately, this has been the problem with the great majority of people everywhere who call themselves Christians. If the tiniest fraction of them were actually Christians, then the radical inner transformation from carnality to divine would invariably reflect in their outward behavior. An individual's outward behavior is the acid test that ultimately reveals weather or not there has truly been an inner transformation

170

of the soul. The fruit of the spirit can only be manifested in the lives of those who have genuinely accepted Christ, and have an intimate relationship with him. Living a true Christian life on earth is a daily experience. Paul said in *Romans Chapter 12*, Verse 1: that the true believer should present his or her body as a living sacrifice. He also said, in *Romans Chapter 12, Verse 2*: "And be ye not conformed to this world; but be ye transformed by the renewing of your mind, that ye may prove what is the good, acceptable, and perfect, will of God." This lets us know that it is a continuous process of growth and development. However, too many calling themselves Christian may have emotionally accepted Jesus Christ as their Savior, but they have never sincerely made him Lord; nor have they honestly endeavored to grow in their knowledge and understanding of Him. This is why they are never victorious over sin in their lives. They remain weak, carnal minded, pseudo-Christians in their ignorance. This is why they are the hapless victims of wickedness and exploitative schemes hatched by those who prey upon the ignorant and the gullible.

God and Satan are in a war for the souls of men. Satan has dominant power and influence over those who are not in Christ. *Ephesians 2:1-2*. He is the architect of this world system of human government that is morally corrupt at its foundation. This is why it does not matter in the least, what particular form of government an individual lives under, it can never guarantee him or her safety, security, or happiness. The blind cannot lead the blind and the lost cannot save the lost. This is why the worldly and carnal mind is enmity toward God. The divine mind is as far from the worldly mind as the east is from the west and as high as the heavens are from the earth. "For my thoughts are not your thoughts, neither are your ways my ways, saith the Lord." "For as the heavens are higher than the earth, so are my ways higher than your ways, and my thoughts than your thoughts". *Isaiah 55:8-9. Matthew Chapter 20, Verses 1-16: and Matthew Chapters 5-7:* Read the Sermon on the Mount. The immortal soul is all that man is, and it holds the potential for all that he can become It is the essence of what, and who, a man is. It is the unmasked character of man. It is his intellect, his will, his passions, and his emotions. In other words, it is his mind, his secret heart, and his innermost self that he fiercely guards, from all but a precious few during his entire lifetime. The soul is the essence of who we really are. It is not what we always proclaim to the out side world. It is that part of us that God knows and it is the basis upon which he ultimately judges us. This is why very few people are brave enough to actually bare their souls to others. They are often ashamed of what and who they really are. Also, they are embarrassed and ashamed of many of the things that they have contemplated and actually done in this life. Therefore, only god ultimately knows the great mass of men and women because only he has the ability to see us for what and who we really are. He can look on us in the eternal and spiritual realm of the soul.

However, those of us living souls who are yet present in our mortal bodies of flesh and blood are limited in our perception of the spiritual world. Therefore, we can only observe one's behavior while in the physical body, and draw conclusions as to the motivations of the soul. On the other hand, any eternal insight into the souls of others that God may grant us through discernment is only given because of our own intimate relationship with him. For without this spiritual discernment, which can only be granted to us at the pleasure of God, those who are crafty enough to hide the true wickedness of their souls often fool us. They do this by displaying the outward appearance of holiness. It is easy for people to pretend that they are holy and sanctified while in church on Sunday. Conversely, this pretense becomes more difficult to maintain throughout the week, especially during those instances when situations and circumstances may challenge temperament and provoke expressions of the true self.

This is why many, who claim to know Christ, are ultimately exposed by their ungodly behavior as hopeless hypocrites. They only have a Sunday morning religion. They are faithful in their church attendance and very active participants in the functioning of their church auxiliaries, but this does not a true Christian make. It is the spirit of Christ and the submission to God's will, that makes one a true Christian. For it is only through an honest and intimate relationship with Christ can the soul be truly transformed in its focus from worldly-minded, self-absorption to divine, Christ- absorption. Once this conversion occurs, holy and righteous living become a natural result which is that spiritual fruit of the true Christian's life. Furthermore, it is impossible for one to do the will of Christ without first, receiving the Holy Spirit of Christ. This indwelling of Christ's spirit is the only way that one can truly be guided by the mind of Christ and move in the power of His authority. Consequently, outside of Christ, the soul can only pursue the lust of the eye, the lust of the flesh, and the pride of life. This is why an individual who has not established a true and intimate relationship with God, can only be a poor facsimile of a Christian.

It is the soul that possesses the courage to search for truth, and has the humility to accept and submit to that truth that Christ is beckoning to eternal life. For it is only through finding that truth about God, the truth that is God, and having the courage to embrace that truth, can we ever hope to be truly free, *John 8:32*. We have been systematically brain washed with lies and myths about us as a people for so long that we have embraced them as truth. However, herein lies the root of our fundamental problem as a people in this nation. It stems directly from the tragic result of generations of Americans being force fed on a steady diet of racist dogma which preaches the inferiority of black skin, and the superiority of white skin. Also, every institution in this nation, governmental, educational, economic, religious, and otherwise, has been established so as to implement and maintain the dictates of this racist doctrine. For centuries in America, every aspect of local and federal governmental policy has been designed to keep black people subordinate to whites in every conceivable area of American life.

Now many white Americans, and even some badly misinformed blacks, have the unmitigated gall to attack affirmative action programs for black Americans. They pontificate with audacious certitude, that blacks will only feel guilty and stigmatized from knowing that they are being given preferential treatment in order to have access to certain business, educational, and professional opportunities. If one would honestly consider the facts in this matter, the inescapable conclusion will reveal that white people have been granted affirmative action and preferential treatment with regard to economic opportunity since the inception of this nation. Ironically, I have never heard any of them lamenting how guilty, depressed, or stigmatized they feel because of their white-skinned privileges and cultural advantages in American society. The white church has been just as guilty as all of those other institutions in degrading, demeaning, and dehumanizing the black man. As I have said before, the black man has been all but totally written out of the Bible and even in those instances where he does appear, his presence is minimized and marginalized. However, when those of us who, through independent research, press harder and dig deeper to find out the truth about God, the black man, and his true role in the scriptures, the findings are usually rejected. Whenever we black scholars unearth anything that has not been sanctioned or approved by white America, it is inevitably other black folk who first, vehemently reject the findings as invalid.

This merely points up the fact of how thoroughly we have been infected with the culturally transmitted disease of innate black skinned inferiority and inherent white skinned superiority. Therefore, precisely who and what we are as a people, has inexorably been shaped by the forces of a culture that rejects, reviles, and vilifies us as sub-human. It regards us as innately inferior to other human beings. It also regards us as insignificant politically, socially, intellectually, and economically, except in those instances when it is advantageous for it to manipulate and exploit us in some way. As a result, we are systematically programmed every day of our lives with information and images designed to reinforce and strengthen the notion of black skinned inferiority and white skinned superiority.

The African-American has been systematically programmed with information filtered through the matrix of western culture to love, desire, and relentlessly pursue that which he is not and to hate, reject, revile, and flee from everything that he is. This is why it is imperative that the intellect, that God given ability to think and reason must be brought to bear in the resolution of our deep-seated psychological problems. The African-American has been taught to believe, especially according to the western interpretation of the Bible, that he is naturally inferior, intellectually limited, and culturally insignificant. Therefore, he is unworthy of any serious recognition in the scriptures. This is why we must have the intellectual honesty to acknowledge truth when we find it and the moral courage to accept that truth after we have found it, even when it requires us to abandon our slavish dedication to this patently racist western mythology of white skinned superiority and black skinned inferiority. As I have stated time and again in this book, the only true and unadulterated version of the Bible is the black man's story. Jesus Christ, himself, was a black man, and so was nearly every single character that appears in the scriptures. The Bible that ninety nine percent of us black Americans read and believe as the gospel truth is nothing, for the most part, but a book of white washed propaganda designed to keep black folk mentally enslaved and locked in that inferior political, economic, and spiritual status designed and defined for us by a racist white culture. We must realize and accept the fact that simply because we have been systematically taught to believe a body of racist dogma of white skinned superiority and black skinned inferiority and have internalized its myths as truth, this does not make the dogma historically valid or even rationally sound.

Therefore, at some point, our intellect must challenge this racist dogma before the just bar with science, logic, and reason. The inescapable verdict will ultimately decree that we have been victimized for centuries by nothing but a wickedly scandalous and colossal lie. We will also find that this vicious lie was concocted and promoted by those who needed a reason to justify their own sadistic barbarity against the black man in an attempt to satisfy their insatiable lust for power, wealth and material comfort. One of our basic problems as a people is that we have been bombarded with so much distorted, convoluted, and patently specious information about God, ourselves, and the world around us, that our souls have been warped and distorted as a consequence. I submit that in order for one to truly know God, he or she has to first know and then be able to accept the unflattering truth about him or herself. On the other hand, I also believe that once one has a true encounter with God, God will stimulate the desire, the passion, and the hunger of the soul to know more about his spiritual truth and more about the natural truth about oneself. If the information available to the soul is distorted, then the soul, influenced by that information, is distorted in terms of how we view ourselves and distorts our basic concept of reality as well. This is precisely what has happened to the black man in America. Therefore, a true desire and sincere hunger to know the truth can be the only salvation of the soul. *John: 32:* "Ye shall know the truth, and the truth shall make you free." *Hosea 4:6:* "My people are destroyed for lack of knowledge." This is why a sincere and intellectually honest investigation into the life of the historical and spiritual Jesus Christ is so important if there is ever going to be any hope of true spiritual redemption for the black church. I contend that it is only through the liberating power of Christ's Holy Spirit, can the black church ever rise above its pathetic religious perpetrating and pseudo-Christian shamming, and begin to fulfill its true purpose on this earth. Anything less than an all out effort to find and then embrace Christ, will result in more of the same spiritual dysfunction and social chaos that is now so rampant in the black church.

Finally, the third and perhaps most important component of man's being, is the spirit. It is the breath of God in man, the life force that gives animation to the physical body. I call this component of man's being the conscience. Some refer to this part of man's being as his spirit. However, I prefer to call it the conscience. This is the component of man's being which is the reflection of his creator. The spirit or conscious is the spark of God in every living being. It is the breath of life that God blew into the nostrils of

Adam, and he became a living soul. It is also that in-born moral compass which provides us all with our most basic sense of right and wrong. It provides us with that in-born and eternal body of information about right and wrong. It is the morally appropriate way that God would have us behave toward Him and our fellowman.

I have often heard old folk refer to the conscience as that still small voice that speaks from within, when one is deliberating some moral decision in the quietness of their own solitude. It is through the spirit or conscience that all men can hear the voice of God. Now whether they choose to listen to and obey that voice or whether they choose not to listen, is another matter. I do believe that babies are born with a conscious and as soon as they can express themselves, they demonstrate a basic knowledge of right and wrong. It is this God conscience in man that makes him feel guilty when he commits an act of wickedness against another. It is the extent to which men listen to and obey this God consciousness that makes them civilized and sane.

This spiritual consciousness is the foundation of moral character in man and it is the basic spiritual structure upon which the pillars of all ethics, principles and morality rest. However, no one is automatically compelled by God to obey the dictates of his conscience. God created man as a free moral agent, with the free will to choose for himself between right and wrong. However, the more a man chooses to obey the moral dictates of his conscience, the easier it becomes for him to do so. Conversely, the more often a man or woman disobeys these eternal dictates of conscience, the easier it becomes to do that also. The scripture refers to those who have seared their consciences by consistently behaving so wickedly, as those who are no longer able to feel guilt or remorse for their evil. Therefore, God has given them over to a reprobated mind, unregenerate and unredeemable in their hopeless wickedness. *Romans 1:28.* We often say of those who seem to be totally oblivious to the gravity of their own wickedness, that they have no conscience. It is possible for men to become so cold and callously wicked in their greed and lust for power, that their consciences can become inoperable. History is replete with examples of man's ruthless savagery against his fellowman. It is possible and often easy for the cold calculated scheming of the intellect and the unbridled passions of the emotions to combine and trample all dictates of conscience. History has shown that many men have stooped in their bottomless evil and perpetrated all manner of ungodly savagery in their quest to rule and dominate their fellowman.

The intellect is often used to plot, plan, scheme, and conjure up all manner of evil and destruction among men. It has been used to concoct every conceivable construct of pseudo-scientific dogma to promote and perpetuate hateful propaganda in man's ungodly efforts to justify his insatiable lust for power and riches. He has used his intellect over the centuries to justify his wickedness and savagery against other men, whose only crime was that they were racially or ethnically different. Consequently, this calculated bestiality has fueled prejudices and inflamed emotions to the extent that all counsel of conscience has been over ruled by flaming passions. This has driven otherwise rational and civilized people to commit the most heinous atrocities against their fellowmen. As a result of hate mongering propaganda which panders to prejudice and ignorance, men and women have historically been, and still are being manipulated and incited to commit the most ruthless barbarity against their fellowmen without the slightest sense of guilt or remorse.

So, throughout the ages, man's intellect, driven by his passions, which have been fueled by greed and the lust for power, has been the greatest enemy of conscience. Simply by his own evil machinations, man has tried to justify his bottomless lust for power and his insatiable greed by creating all manner of myths in his vain attempt to cast his victims as subhuman or irretrievably wicked. He has tried to use his intellect in an attempt to justify his own savagery against them, and then absolve himself of any moral guilt. It is this conscience, this higher God-self in us, that makes us human; it is the only thing that makes us human. Therefore, history has shown us that when conscience is repressed or abandoned, the results for human societies are catastrophic. So, it is this conscience, this higher God-self in man that enables him to behave morally appropriate toward his fellowman. Nevertheless as I have already stated, man is not bound to listen to, and obey the dictates of his conscience. Although, the more he does, the more he finds that he is able to do so. Therefore, this conscious mind can be strengthened in terms of its influence on one behavior. The more one behaves right and just, the easier it becomes to do so. Conversely, the harder it becomes to do that which is wrong or wicked.

Consequently, right behavior cultivates and strengthens the influence of conscience and wrong behavior weakens and diminishes the influence of conscience.

So the ultimate case of whether a man will be good or evil will depend on his adherence to, or abandonment of his conscience. In other words, whether a man listens to and then obeys the voice of his own conscious determines whether he will behave in a good or evil way. It is through this spiritual conscience that we are aware of that divine and eternal mind of God at all. Again, whether or not we choose to acknowledge Him is another matter. However, whatever decision one makes will ultimately reflect itself in outward behavior. It is this spiritual conscience, that higher God-self, that is the only real potential for any good in man. However, outside of a genuine acceptance of, and an intimate relationship with Jesus Christ as Lord and Savior, there can be neither remission for man's sins nor redemption for his lost soul. So, the popular notion of being a good and morally just man is not enough to inherit the kingdom of heaven. Jesus Christ requires that one must confess with their mouth and believe in their heart that God hath raised him from the dead, thou shalt be saved, *Rom.10:9*.

So it is through this God conscience in us that allows us to know what we do know about the personality of God, and how to take the right and proper action toward each other. For it is this divine God conscience with which we emerge from the womb that endows us with the capacity to be human and civilized. It is our in-born moral compass that points us to that eternal pole of just, moral, and righteous human behavior. It is our only eternal, immutable, and divinely sanctioned frame of reference for human existence. It is the only thing that significantly separates human kind from all other animals on the planet. God gave man a conscience, a part of Himself, and then made him master over the earth. However, it has been the systematic searing and ruthless trampling of this conscience which has made men sink to levels of barbarity rivaling the most savage beasts.

This is why it is so important that the church appeals to the consciences of men and simultaneously be that clarion voice which vehemently challenges the unethical, immoral, unprincipled and most ungodly behavior of men. For it is the rehabilitation of conscience that leads men and women to the realization that they need God. Furthermore, it is through the maintenance of conscience that men and women can honestly come to grips with themselves and realize how far from God that they really are. For it is through this conscience that God communicates with us. It is the medium and means by which He allows us to know Him and know His will, even if we choose not to listen or obey Him. When a man or woman is in the right relationship with God, it will be through this conscience that He will lead and guide them. The behavior of a good man, a wise man, and a God fearing man is governed by the mind of god, which he perceives by way of his conscience.

It was this conscience that motivated some white Americans living in the Antebellum south under the awful institution of human slavery, to defy law, custom, and convention and treat black men and women like fellow human beings. Many of these white people, like the great John Brown, lost their own lives because of their efforts to free those held in slavery. They were compelled by conscience to do what was right, moral, and just, in the eyes of God, despite the fact that the great majority of their countrymen were willing to submit to the tyranny of their laws, customs, and convention. They were willing to give their lives for what they knew was right, even while millions of their fellow countrymen chose to bow down to one of the most wicked systems of human degradation ever conceived in the minds of men. Likewise, their were many German citizens who again were compelled by conscience to defy Hitler's Nazi Germany and risk their own lives in order to save the lives of thousands of Jews who had been condemned to death in crematoriums. This unspeakably horrible slaughter of fellow human beings, which began as early as 1932, was actually brazenly carried on by a so- called, "Christian and literate nation". What is even more damnable is that the ruthless extermination of Jews, Gypsies, and other so-called undesirable minorities, was conducted in the eyes of the entire world without even the feeblest protest from other nations. There was no military action taken against Nazi Germany on the part of a single nation in an attempt to halt this senseless mass-murder, until 1939 when Germany attacked Poland.

Sadly, since the close of World War II, this same pattern of systematic extermination of minorities has persisted with shameful regularity all over the globe. It has taken place in Africa, Asia, Europe, the

Middle East, and in South America, just to name a few places. However, the rest of the "Civilized Christian Nations", have simply turned their collective heads and looked the other way. There have always been a few people living in those nations that have created systems of social oppression of minority groups of which they were not a part, but they have been willing to place their own lives in jeopardy to help those who were being oppressed. These are those people who have cultivated their consciences to such a high degree throughout their lives, that they are compelled to go against the popular sentiment or social convention, even though their decisions may bring retribution or even death to them or their families.

These are those who have embraced the eternal dictates of conscience that the oneness of God confirms the oneness of man: that it is far easier to be moral than immoral, far easier to be ethical than unethical and far easier to be principled than to be unprincipled. There are also those who know that the ethnic and cultural differences between men, despite what the racists proclaim, are purely biologically superficial, because all men are basically the same. However, the differences between men and beasts are profound, especially when there is the presence of conscience. Take away conscience and the behavior of men and beasts becomes identical. It is the conscience, the God-self in us which tells us the human and civilized thing that we ought to do, which is not always what we may want to do. So it is this eternal spark of God in man that gives him the opportunity

185

to be divine, or despicable, benevolent, or malevolent, an angel, or a devil.

It is conscience or the lack there of, that makes us all who and what we really are. Therefore, the church is the place where conscience should be cultivated and strengthened in order to make men and women reach their fullest potential in Christ. However, it would be folly to expect this kind of honest and sincere examination of conscience to be under taken by the current crop of spiritually dysfunctional church leadership. On the contrary, they are for the most part too bereft of conscience to be of any significant use. Those who have healthy consciences must tackle the task of conscience cultivation. A man must first be acquainted with honesty, integrity, and genuine compassion before he can ever be a credible example of these things. Those who have, intact and healthy consciences, must exhibit the vitally important examples of conscience. Otherwise, they will only succeed in demonstrating more of the same old blatant hypocrisy and pathetic delusion that is the present stock and trade of the black church in particular and so called, "Christian Church" in general.

So, this will be a job for only those who are qualified and equipped to teach, not only by precept, but also, and more importantly, by living example. It is conscience, the god-self in man, that is the only hope for man's reclamation and elevation from beast to human and his salvation from sinner to saint on this earth. Conscience is the only means by which man can know and do what is right, just, honest and true. Therefore, this conscience, this spirit, this god-self in man, cannot and must not continue to be omitted in black church teaching. Man is body, soul, and spirit or conscience. These three equally crucial components of man's being must be thoroughly examined and systematically reexamined, if the black church is ever going to even come close to the true holistic view of man as a living being who is created in the image of God.

It will be this kind of honest, sincere, uncompromising, unadulterated, spiritually and historically sound teaching of Christianity that will enable the black church to be a spiritual light house in the African-American community. It can finally allow the black man to shed his mental shackles of self- hatred and break his pattern of self-destructive behavior. Then, he can step forth into the bright sunshine of psychological wholeness and spiritual freedom.

CHAPTER 11

What is the Seat of the Problem Concerning the Proper education of African-American Children?

The cultural genocide and psychologically malignant effect of the living Legacy of North American Slavery on the minds of African-Americans, has never been honestly addressed by mainstream academia, much less, seriously analyzed. The Trans-Atlantic slave trade began around 1450 and lasted until the mid 1800's. The nations of Europe discovered the vast continents of North America and Africa around the same time. These nations subsequently engaged in fierce competition to establish colonies and gain a foothold in the "New World." However, they were unable to convince enough of their own citizens to migrate to such a strange and far off place, especially not in sufficient numbers necessary for economic exploitation and cultural conquest of the vast new continent. As a result, these nations looked to Africa to satisfy this need. Nearly every nation in Europe participated in the heinous enterprise known as the Trans-Atlantic slave trade. They quickly established forts along the western coast of Africa and often fought savagely with each other for control and domination of the extremely lucrative trafficking in human flesh.

England was the dominant sea power during this period. Consequently, she was the primary actor in the slave trade. Merchant ships from England, along with those of other European nations, relentlessly swarmed the western coast of Africa, dumping cheaply manufactured goods in exchange for black bodies. When they had depleted the supply of Africans living along the coast, these Europeans then moved further inland in order to maintain their profitable trade in black bodies. They eagerly supplied certain African kings with lead, powder, and European arms to enable them to make war on their neighbors so they could maintain the abundant supply of slaves to the whites. This strategy of pitting African rulers against each other caused a chain reaction of relentless conflict which rapidly enveloped the entire continent. The reason that the Trans-Atlantic slave trade lasted so long was because it was extremely profitable. Therefore, the European's insatiable demand for Africa's black bodies, to feed their bottomless greed for wealth and unquenchable lust for power, fueled the Trans-Atlantic slave trade for four and a half centuries. It was the European's answer to cheap labor in the "New World."

The Europeans exploited every possible ethnic, tribal, cultural, and national difference already existing among the Africans in order to stimulate and maintain a steady supply of slaves. Armed with superior European weapons and the allure of more of Europe's manufactured goods, African kings made constant war upon each other in order to acquire more slaves for the Trans-Atlantic trade. Whole villages were raided and the populations of entire communities were decimated during this relentless warring among African kings in their effort to obtain more and more bodies for the slave trade. When the supply of black victims had been depleted along the coast, Africans were then hunted and captured far into the interior of the continent. Then they were marched to the coast where they were kept in fortified forts, owned by the various European nations. There these tragic souls were chain together, fed in troughs like pigs, and housed in pens until ships arrived to dump their trade goods and pick up the waiting human cargo. The African captives were clamped into irons, crammed into the hulls of sailing ships like cordwood, and taken thousands of miles away from their homes, never to return. They were brought to North America, South America, and distributed throughout the Caribbean. These African captives were brought to seasoning plantations where they were ruthlessly and systematically stripped of every vestige of their culture and humanity, then reduced to personal property and turned into beasts of burden. They were totally stripped of their language, religion, and every cultural value and belief that had made them who, and what they had been for centuries. Then they were methodically terrorized, sadistically brutalized, and ruthlessly degraded on a scale that would shock even the most sadistic mine.

This is how their white "Christian" masters systematically stripped them of their humanity and turned them into Negroes, or personal property. The enslaved Africans were unilaterally excommunicated from the human family by the Europeans and redefined as Negroes. Then they were culturally relegated to the legal status of personal property. In other words, their legal status was no different from that of other domesticated animals: horses, cattle, sheep, hogs, dogs, and chickens. Consequently, Europeans bought and sold these Negro slaves in the marketplace, just like they did other common livestock.

After each shipload of African captives arrived at these, "New World", seasoning plantations, and they had been thoroughly stripped of their language, religion, and every other trace of their native culture, the natural generational transmission of this knowledge was totally extinguished. Consequently, the unfortunate progeny of these African captives were completely robbed of their natural African heritage and cultural identity. In other words, because all of the knowledge of their fore-parent's culture had been so barbarically suppressed and systematically extinguished, the tragic descendants of these victims had no possible way of knowing their true African heritage or genuine ethnic identity. In other words, the unfortunate offspring of these original African slaves had no earthly idea of whom, or what they really were. As a result, the minds of these children of those originally enslaved Africans provided the blank slates upon which these egomaniacal white masters created the world's first real Frankenstein monster, the Negro.

The Negro was only created to produce unlimited wealth and comfort for his master and to free him from all physical labor. Therefore, the Negro or chattel slave's only purpose was to submit to his master's every whim and serve at his owner's selfish pleasure. So the unfortunate slave's mind was a clean slate to be written upon by those whose aim was only to justify their ruthless savagery and subjugation of the African captive, by redefining him as a Negro, slave, or piece of personal property. However, this self-serving, capricious, and totally arbitrary redefinition of the African from fellow human being to personal property, was concocted by these "Christian" Europeans in order to release them from all natural constraints of human conscious or dictates of ethicality as a result of their heinous treatment of the African. Consequently, the European's dubious concoction of the ridiculously absurd myth of black skinned inferiority and white skinned superiority, was absolutely necessary in order to justify his unconscionably savage behavior toward the African. So the European elite imposed upon their scholars in every discipline, to push their pseudo-science and faulty logic to absurd extremes in their insane attempt to create an inter-disciplinary dogma to validate their scurrilous and totally arbitrary assertion of black skinned innate inferiority to white skinned people.

So in truth, it was their own unspeakably barbaric and morally indefensible behavior toward the African that motivated them to create such baseless dogma, no matter how scientifically preposterous, logically absurd, or morally translucent. This frantic obsession of the Europeans to define the African as an inferior creature, had to be done, or science and logic would have had to decree by every principle of reason, cannon of morality, or standard of civilized behavior, that the unmitigatedly barbarity of these Europeans, themselves, toward fellow human beings, represented the absolute epitome of moral bankruptcy and unmitigated mass insanity. Consequently, these Europeans were obliged to create this ridiculous body of myth and superstition about the African in their malevolent attempt to confirm his innate inferiority, in order to hide their own hideous bestiality and justify their own sadistic barbarity against him. Moreover, this horrific crime against humanity was perpetrated primarily to satisfy the European's insatiable greed for profit, and unquenchable lust for power. Therefore, the white master was neither bound by any restraint of morality, nor constrained by any dictate of conscious in his insidious effort to reduce the African to a piece of property, an order to make possible, his acquisition of wealth and power. This was the primary goal of all teaching and training of the enslaved African. The slaves were taught, by terrifying example and practical daily precept, three cardinal principles. First of all, they were indoctrinated with an all-consuming fear of their omnipotent master's in particular and all white people in general. Next they were taught that they were bound to submit to, and automatically obey their master's every demand, without any hint of question or complaint. Then the slaves were systematically indoctrinated with a profound sense of their own innate inferiority to whites and forced to adopt a specific set of behavior patterns designed to consistently confirm and re-enforce their cultural inferiority to whites and subordinate status to them.

The American Negro has been subjected to a physiologically unique and psychologically horrendous experience, chattel slavery which is without parallel in human history. Furthermore, this physical and psychologically dehumanizing experience lasted for four and a half centuries. The kind of ruthless subjugation and sadistic brutality that was systematically inflicted upon African slaves in the Americas and throughout the Caribbean, for more than four and a half centuries is certainly without parallel in the annals of world history. Therefore as a result of this horrendous experience, the African mind has yet to recover its original native ethnic, cultural, and spiritual equilibrium. Consequently, the ex-slave remains tragically estranged from his original Africanness: his true black soul, his natural African mind, and his proper ethnic identity. Most white people are ashamed to honestly discuss the truth about the African holocaust during the four and a half centuries of black chattel slavery. Moreover, most black people are ashamed to acknowledge the fact that they are still inexorably spiritually, mentally, psychologically, and economically crippled because of four and a half centuries of this horrendous black victimization.

Furthermore, most blacks, especially the black bourgeoisie, are desperately afraid to talk open and honestly about it, for fear of offending their white social or economic benefactors. Nevertheless, the glaring fact cannot be disputed or discounted, that the Negro has endured a kind of systematically and methodically barbaric physical and psychological subjugation that has left him culturally estranged from Africa, and psychologically alienated from himself. In other words, he is neither European, nor African. He has been taught to revile, reject, and despise everything that nature, objectively declares that he is. Conversely, he has been taught to love, worship, prize, and idolize everything European, but that he knows, in his secret heart, that he is not and can never be. He calls himself an American, because

194

he has had every trace of his native African culture and heritage beaten out of him, and for four and a half centuries, he has been indoctrinated with his master's culture. As a result, he has been forced to embrace and internalize a culture which has systematically degraded, dehumanized, rejected, and reviled him. Consequently, as a result of four and a half centuries of European cultural indoctrination, he perceives himself as having more in common with his slave master, than he does his natural African kin. The tragic fact remains, that the legacy of chattel slavery has left the Negro culturally destitute, psychologically impotent, and spiritually dead. He still frantically pursues everything that he is not, and flees from everything that he is. Sadly, he still longs for acceptance from those who enslaved, degraded, and dehumanized him, then reduced him to a piece of personal property, to be bought and sold in the marketplace. Moreover, he still searches for identity in a culture that has inferiorized him, made him a Frankenstein Monster, and has defined him as personal property and a commercial commodity. As a result, he yet wonders aimlessly in a spiritual, cultural, and psychological no-man's land of intellectual impotence, spiritual annihilation, and systematic self-destruction. He has no native land, no native language, religion, or culture, except that which has been externally imposed upon him by his slave master. However, this is a hostile and alien culture which has historically viewed and continues to view him as naturally inferior to white skinned people. Therefore, he is regarded as being unworthy and not deserving of the same common human rights or citizenship prerogatives

195

that white skinned people take for granted in Western European dominated societies.

"If you do not understand white supremacy: what it is, and how it works, everything else that you think that you understand, will only confuse you." (Neely Fuller Jr. 1971: *"the United Independent compensatory code System Concept"*) Dr. Francis Cress Welsing suggests that, "White people, or the incidence of white skin is actually a recessive genetic trait, and really an occurrence of albinism. European people have long realize this unalterable scientific fact and have consequently established a global system of domination and control over all people whom they have classified as non-white. Their primary motivation for organizing and implementing such a system of global domination and control, was to protect themselves from biological annihilation by non-white people." (Francis Cress Welsing: *"The Isis Papers"*, 1991) It is hard for any reputable scholar to refute the fact that at least, for the past two thousand years, the white race, or European has dominated the affairs of the globe. In his book, *"The United Independent Compensatory Code Concept"*, Neely Fuller contends that the white supremacist has gained domination and control of nine primary areas of life, of all the world's people that they have classified as non-white. Fuller asserts that the areas of: sex, religion, economics, war, law, education, entertainment, labor, and politics, are all thoroughly and totally dominated and controlled by the world's elite white collective Consequently, he maintains that it is that global white collective which defines and dictates the reality for all non-white people. Fuller further suggest

196

that, Western European Culture is nothing more than another name for white supremacy. It has inundated, saturated, and permeated the entire globe. This white Western European collective enforces its will through its technology and Science. Moreover, it holds a monopoly on the technological powers of mass destruction, which it sees as its means of dominating and controlling the non-white population of the globe. Furthermore, it has a strangle hold on the world's wealth which it also uses to dominate and control the affairs of all non-white people.

The white supremacist clearly understands and appreciates the fact that the black man is his archenemy. Why, because the black man has the greatest capacity to produce melanin, and consequently has the greatest potential to inflict white skinned biological annihilation. This is why the white supremacists are so rabid in their determination to control the black man. Invariably, this is why they originally created and have maintained the whole body of dogmatic myth and superstition about the black man's innate inferiority, in their relentless attempts to marginalize and demonized him in order to justify their ruthless suppression and economic exploitation of him. Consequently, the white supremacists have found it necessary to historically cast the African as a demon, a devil, a savage brute, and a sub-human beast, in their desperate effort to absorb themselves of their own sadistic barbarity that they have systematically perpetrated against him. So not only do America, but also the whole world turns on the axes of white supremacy. Western culture, from its inception, has provided the white supremacist with a whole range of values and beliefs endemic to his class. It has also equipped him with a set of very rigid and systematized patterns of conscious and unconscious behaviors toward non-white peoples, designed to maintain and insure the white collective's status of global domination.

Finally, if the Negro is not operating from this premise, then he has failed to grasp an understanding of the white supremacist's basic perception of the world and the basis upon which his primary motives and actions rest. Consequently, he will never make any significant progress in countering the profoundly destructive effects of white supremacy imposed upon him and his kind. For it is only by understanding this stupendously insidious phenomenon, can one predict or counter its effects.

The miseducation of the Negro, since his creation on the plantation, must be viewed in the Context of White Supremacy. Our esteemed Educator and writer, Carter G. Woodson, argues that, "The Negro is taught to admire the European, to marvel at his Accomplishments, but to despise Africa." (Carter G. Woodson: *"The Miseducation of the Negro"*, 1933). As I have fore stated, the African was taken from his homeland, forced into slavery, and turned into a Negro. He was never supposed to be anything more than a means of acquiring wealth and a source of cheap labor for his white master. Therefore, he was never actually educated, but merely indoctrinated or trained. He was obliged to learn just enough to make him an easily manageable and efficient servant for his master. Therefore, the slave was trained just as one would train a hunting dog, a horse, or a mule merely to perform a specific function or service. Therefore, the Negro or black slave was trained to behave specifically according to his predetermined role as an economic tool in the context of White Western European Culture. True education involves, not only equipping one with the cultural knowledge to survive, but the ability to think, reason, theorize, and problem solve. This kind of genuine, rigorous, mind-developing education has never been provided for Negroes in America, before or evens since, the end of chattel slavery. Renowned black scholar and teacher, Dr. Ni-am Akbar, asserts that, "The black man's place in America was to be that of a permanent slave and servant to his white master. This is why he has been historically taught so expertly, to hate, revile, and utterly despise himself, and everything black or African." Dr. Akbar further contends that, " White folk actually hate our children. Moreover, they have skillfully taught many of our black teachers to hate our children too. This is why they have concluded that black children cannot learn." (Dr. Na-am Akbar, Lecture: Columbus Ohio 1995)

Education for the white child in America has meant one thing, but education for the black child has meant something entirely different. For example, the white child is taught that his ancestors were proud, brave, and noble people, who conquered heathen savages and developed this continent into the great nation that it is today. However, the black child learns that his ancestor's only role in the settling of this continent was that of chattel slaves, beasts of burden, and a source of cheap labor. The white child can point with pride, to all the scientific inventions of his people which sparked the industrial revolution, and industrial development of this nation. However, the black child must stand feeling ashamed, inadequate, and mute on this matter. Why, because the thousands of scientific inventions by blacks have been stolen by whites or simply written out of the history books. Unfortunately, this kind of critical confidence-building information is absent from most school curriculums, even those large urban school districts with majority black enrollments. The white child is introduced to the music, art, and literature of Europe and hears it referred to as classical. Conversely, the black child hears nothing about the classical music, art, and literature of Africa which predates that of Europe by centuries. The ironic and perverted fact is, that the music, art, and literature of Africa have provided the very structural and theoretical foundation upon which all so-called Classical European music, art, and literature are based.

Finally, the mass brain-washing that has been called the," Education" of black children in this nation, has been nothing more than a fraud, a sham, and a cruel joke for centuries. This same incalculably deleterious effect on black children has still held true, even when the educational process has been in the hands of black administrators, themselves. Why, because the primary creation and development of the educational curriculum for black children has historically been, and continues to remain, firmly in the hands of whites. Therefore, it continues to be created, designed, and executed thoroughly within the context and goal of the philosophy of white supremacy

200

Despite the fact that, in some cases, blacks may be administering the educational bureaucracy, whites invariably design the teaching curriculum and instructional objectives which ultimately dictate America's fundamental educational policy.

Consequently, this policy is certainly implemented within the context and ultimately conforms to the primary goals and objectives of white supremacy. As a result, there is a stylized and systematic maintenance of the status quo of white supremacy: black skinned inferiority and white skinned superiority. The poignant evidence of this sad fact is, that these vaunted black administered school districts, still cannot produce any significant numbers of authentic or bona fide critical thinkers, scientific problem solvers, or bona fide political or economic theoreticians, who can seriously address the pathetic economic, social, political, and spiritual plight of blacks in America. So the great majority of these public school districts and even colleges administered by blacks, have failed miserably, to produce sufficient academicians equipped to effectively tackle the myriad of protracted and debilitating ills afflicting black people in this nation. The evidence is painfully clear that under the cultural domination of white supremacy, American education, even in the hands of blacks, can never produce a truly black consciousness or African brain trust, but only a black brain drain.

In other words, our best minds are quickly co-opted by white organizations or business concerns as soon as there is the slightest glimmer of genius, to work for those who still economically exploit and politically oppress us. This is why it is this writer's assertion that black folk educated under white supremacy can only, but be trained as functionaries for the maintenance of the system of white domination. According to esteemed black teacher and Psychologists, Dr. Amos N. Wilson, author of, *"The Developmental Psychology of the Black Child"*, "The notion of being an American, can not possibly mean the same for black and white children." He maintains that, "The African-American's experience of slavery in the United States, is not the white American's experience of slave mastery." Dr. Wilson further contends that, "A whole psychology comes from these two histories, a whole set of attitudes, a whole way of seeing the world and dealing with the world comes from these two histories. Consequently, both simply saying that they are Americans, does not resolve the differences or the psychology of these two histories."(Amos N. Wilson. *"The Developmental Psychology of the Black Child"*;(1990). This only under scores this writers contention that the purpose of what we call education in America was never design to equip black or even white children with the intellectual skills to think critically, analytically, or even problem solve. On the contrary, it was, and is designed to produce compliant, quiescent, docile, and self-indulgent Negroes who know their place, and are more willing to stay in it.

This is a tragic testament as to why there has been pitifully little rigorous analysis or serious dissertation concerning the horrendous cultural, malignant psychological, pathetic economic and terminal spiritual impact of white supremacy on black people. Except for a handful of courageous black scholars, who have been relentlessly ridiculed and castigated by white counterparts; who are to afraid and ashamed to deal with the catastrophic implications of this black holocaust themselves, black academia has simply stood weak-kneed, lily-livered, and cowardly mute on the subject. America is home to the single most "educated" technologically advanced and wealthiest group of black people on this planet. They have ready access to the greatest centers of scientific and technological learning in the world, yet they lack the courage or the will to utilize this incredible scientific research and technology to resolve some of their own chronic and debilitating economic and social problems. Paradoxically, America's, black elite has failed miserably, to produce any valid or replicable economic models, creditable psychological paradigms, or workable social constructs sufficient to counter the withering effects of white supremacy upon the minds of black people in this nation. Furthermore, it poignantly underscores the sorry fact that there is no moral imperative upon this ethnically alienated and brain-dead black bourgeoisie to seriously endeavor to improve the social, economic, and political plight of the masses of poor black people here in America, or non-white peoples around the world. Our esteemed Elder E. Franklin Frazier suggested that this black bourgeoisie was merely created in the first place, and only allowed to exist to function as a buffer class between the white elite and lower classed black masses. This vaunted class's main function is that of overseer, or the proscribed administrator of the black community. In other words, this black bourgeoisie has been expertly trained by the white supremacists, through generations of indoctrination to suppress any inkling of independent black thought and native aspirations of economic self- determination and maintain the racists white elite's economic, political, and social status quo, at all cost. As a result, this hopelessly reactionary, morally bereft, spiritually dead, and intellectually dysfunctional class of unctuous sycophants has historically been, and continues to be, the most effective tool in our community for the maintenance of black misery and white supremacy.

CHAPTER 12

Five Main Points in James Baldwin's Article: "A Message to Teachers"

It is this writer's humble opinion that James Baldwin's five major points to teachers as stipulated in his article are: teachers must be revolutionaries, the conventional function of education, the true purpose of education, the white man's disconnection with reality, and the social paradox of the black student. Mr. Baldwin concedes that these issues have combined to place a stupendous burden on the shoulders of those of us who are sincerely interested in the true education of America's children. The gravity of the problem of miseducation of all American children, as Mr. Baldwin has articulated it, has been so pervasive and deeply rooted in our culture, that it will demand nothing less than a total commitment of purpose and absolute dedication of effort on the part of us, who even hope to make a difference in rectifying so monumental a malady.

Mr. Baldwin seems to feel that we, who choose to be teachers, must first understand that, we must be revolutionaries. We must be willing to embrace the notion that we will have to challenge the status quo with our conviction to teach the truth about the world around us and about ourselves. However, this will inevitably bring us into direct conflict with a deeply entrenched and thoroughly intractable educational bureaucracy which will certainly seek to crush us for daring to step outside of its vaunted convention. Consequently, there will be an avalanche of opposition to our attempt to change the focus and goal of education. We will certainly be branded as troublemakers, militants, malcontents, rebel-rousers, and much worst. As a result, these charges which, no doubt, will be leveled by those who want to maintain the status quo of shameful miseducation, will carry serious penalties for us who seek to inject a modicum of sanity into the process. Consequently, it will certainly cost us in our effort to advance a rational, critical, and honest approach to teaching into this pathetic behemoth of mass insanity, now called American education. Therefore, we must resolve at the outset, to be firm and steadfast in the depth of our conviction to what we believe is the true purpose and ultimate goal of education. Moreover, we must be absolutely resolute in the strength of our determination to stand on our convictions, no matter what the personal and professional cost.

Next Mr. Baldwin contends that the conventional function of education is to civilize an individual – in other words, to train him or her as to how to fit, or assume his or her role in a particular society. For example, education is supposed to enable an individual to understand what his or her place is, and to stay in his or her place. Furthermore, its purpose is to teach and train an individual to respect and uphold the laws, values, beliefs, and general philosophy of the society in which he or she lives. However, Mr. Baldwin admits that this is, in no way, the true purpose of education far from it. It is the true educator's job to produce individuals who have an unvarnished or objective concept of themselves and the world. These are those who can analyze and synthesize information for themselves, then reach their own conclusions about things. Those who by virtue of their teaching and training, will be provided with a range of analytical paradigms which will enable them, not only to answer questions, but more importantly, to question the traditional answers. Therefore, they will be able to reach their own conclusions about their society and the world, based on sound logic and rational analysis, predicated on verifiable empirical evidence.

Consequently, such an individual cannot so easily be dominated or manipulated by the political demagogues and economic elites of the society. As a result of this capacity to think critically, analyze and synthesize phenomena and draw conclusions based on independent analysis, he or she may become a threat to the status quo. Sometimes, this kind of critical and analytically thinking individual is viewed as undesirable and even dangerous to the maintenance of the social, political, and economic stability of a society. We have witnessed this insidious phenomenon time an again during the Civil Rights Movement, with outright governmental assault on individuals like: Malcolm X, Martin Luther King, Bobby Sills, H. Rap Brown, Huey P. Newton, and a whole host of others, who dared to challenge the ugly contradictions, which is the racist status quo of American society. They demanded that America, stop perpetrating as a paragon of freedom and democracy to the rest of the world, while she was busy propping up some of the most brutal and repressive governments on the planet. They also demanded that America honestly address, and then correct her pathetic hypocrisy of posturing as a free nation while simultaneously practicing a racial apartheid, right within her own borders. They challenged America to acknowledge the glaring ethical discrepancies between her pompous preachments of freedom and democracy and her scandalous practice of racial oppression, and finally live up to her Constitutional guarantees of equal citizenship rights and privileges for all Americans.

Furthermore, even before the advent of the Civil Rights Movement, America has historically ostracized, vilified, or simply destroyed any black man or woman who dared to advocate and agitate for equal citizenship rights and privileges for black people in this nation. Just a cursory survey of American history will reveal how the economic and political power elite of this nation has relentlessly and systematically demonized, marginalized, and vilified those courageous black leaders like: Martin Luther King, Elijah Mohammed, Marcus Garvey, W.E.B. DuBois, Frederick Douglas, Malcolm X, Paul Robeson, Martin Dulaney, and all others who dared to agitate for the full citizenship rights and privileges of black folks in America. Mr. Baldwin contends that the white man is totally disconnected from reality because he has created a body of myth about himself and every one else. He sees himself as a hero and looks at the whole world through the grossly distorted perception of his own deified image and his idealized culture. As a result, he views himself as being innately superior to all the world's people that he has arbitrarily classified as non-white, and therefore he has been divinely anointed to dominate and exploit them. So the racists' myth of his white skinned superiority and all other non-white peoples as being inherently inferior, has been thoroughly woven into the very matrix of his ethnocentric culture.

Consequently, he has created a totally false identity for himself. However, this identity is totally based on his flimsy foundation of myth and superstition, which he has concocted in order to justify his ruthless brutality and bottomless savagery against the world's non-white peoples. This is why he sees his own grotesquely distorted culture and history as all-important and the cultures and histories of all other peoples that he has classified as being non-white as trivial and inferior to his own. Consequently, in his fanatic attempt to legitimize his own culture and history, he has decided that they are the only subject areas worthy of his attention and study. So, he has grotesquely mythologized his own history and culture and conversely, trivialized and even vilified the histories and cultures of all other non-white peoples'. This insidious culpability is nowhere more poignant, than in the case of the black man. The white man, in his ruthless subjugation and domination of the black man, has been obliged to pervert and subvert every sacrosanct moral and ethical precept of rational thought imperative to civilized society.

Moreover, he has created all manner of pseudo-scientific dogma, in his absurd and relentless determination to declare the black man as sub-human, therefore innately inferior to himself. As a result, he has been able to convince himself that his sadistic barbarity against the African has not actually been perpetrated against fellow human beings, but a race of primeval beast which did not possess immortal souls, intellect, or other natural human affections. So this reprobated belief has apparently freed the European from the unconscionable guilt that would be naturally engendered by his bottomless barbarity against fellow human beings, by arbitrarily redefining his victims as subhuman. As a result, his behavior became psycho parasitic, in that his own identity and concept of self, and self- worth, is directly tied to his belief in the natural inferiority of the black man, and the natural superiority of himself to all non-white or non-Western European peoples. In other words, this was the primary notion upon which the initial concept of white skinned psychological and political identity was originally predicated, and the sole psychological construct upon which it has rested ever since. Consequently, the white man actually does not know who, or what he is, without his symbiotic dependence upon his body of dogmatic myths and vulgar superstitions, that he has concocted concerning the supposedly base or primeval nature of the black man. So this is the insidiously self-serving strategy that he has created and promoted over the centuries, ostensibly to confirm in him, a sense of his own innate superiority to the black man in particular, and all other peoples of which he has classified as non-European or non-white on the planet in general.

Ironically, this dogmatic body of myth and superstition about the black man's innate inferiority, that the white man has so meticulously created, when placed under rational scrutiny and sober analysis, only exposes the European as the real intellectual
210

fraud and monstrous beast himself. The inescapable verdict of logic and critical analysis invariably indicts the white man as being totally bereft of all of the lofty trappings of humanity and, "Christian civilization" that he has so pompously proclaimed to the world, that he possesses. This is also a part of the monumental task which lays ahead for those who wish to truly educate America's children. We not only have to educate black children, but the white children too, for they are also just as sorely miseducated.

Finally, Mr. Baldwin laments about the paradox which confronts the black child with regards to the kind of education he has traditionally received. First of all, he is made to feel proud that he lives in a nation that has never lost a war, or been dominated by another nation. Furthermore, he is made to feel proud with regards to the phenomenal technological and mechanistic accomplishments that America has made over the centuries. Paradoxically, American history also tells the black child that he and his kind, has had absolutely no significant role in any of these great accomplishments. He is obliged to concede that his history is one of degradation, humiliation, and shame. Conventional education has taught him that, he and his kind, has factored into the building of America into such a great world power, only in their pathetic role as human chattel.

Consequently, the black child has been obliged to accept the fact that he and his people's contribution to the emergence of America as a dominant world power, has been that of slaves and a source of cheap labor for brilliant pioneering and trail blazing white folk.

Furthermore, he is obliged to except the tragically sobering fact that any one but him and his kind can become president of this nation. Moreover, he may look with admiration upon those white folk who have managed to rise above their meager circumstances and become captains of industry and major economic forces in various aspects of American life, but he knows because of his black skin, and those deep-seated cultural prejudices, stereotypes, and myths about him and his kind, such possibilities are virtually off limits to him. As a result, the black youth becomes just like so many of his fellows, hopelessly apathetic about his life prospects, becomes an escapist through alcohol and drugs, or seriously thoughtful, reflective, and very angry about the injustice that this racist and oppressive white society imposes upon him. As a result of his critical and reflective thinking, he may become a seething mass of pent up rage. However, he dares not express or direct that rage at white folk, whom he knows is the source of it, but he must always be polite, courteous, and treat them with the utmost deference and respect.

Why? Because he realizes that they are in total control of this society and as a result, they hold the ultimate power of life and death over him. Never the less, white folk remain the very personification of his oppression, and their economically successful lives, juxtaposed to his own grinding poverty, becomes the very mirror of his denied opportunity. So it is the stupendous task of us who are educators to teach and train both black and white children to think and reason for themselves. We must equip our children with the sufficient critical and analytical thinking skills to

212

see America and American society for what it really is. However more importantly, we must instill in them, the courage to be the kind of future revolutionaries, who will be willing to challenge this mass insanity which is America's institutional racism, that has traditionally been and yet remains, the status quo of American miseducation.

CHAPTER 13

The Politics of Intelligence Testing: Pseudo-Science used to Justify White Supremacy

The worst blight on scientific research and inquiry during the past century has been the pathetic extent to which white supremacists have been willing to stoop, in the name of science, in their scurrilous obsession to advance their racist dogma, cloaked in the guise of scientific validity. Their scandalous effort has been nowhere more devastating, than in the area of shaping America's educational policy for black and other non-white children. From the myriad of race based intelligence and achievement test, to the body of pseudo-science created to justify and buttress the deleterious effects of these test, white supremacists have stoop to the absolute depths of pseudo-scientific absurdity in their fiendish obsession to oppress blacks and other non-white racial minorities in America.

Even the most naive mind can not escape the fact that standardized test have long been used in this nation as a means of social control. However, this insidious method of savagely circumscribing black upward economic mobility has been successful because the creation and implementation of educational policy for blacks in America has been solely at the hands of white elite's. Therefore, for decades they have used this standardized testing strategy to justify their discriminatory educational decisions against black children.

214

Ironically, they were able to convince those of us who were directly affected, that their information for making such damaging decisions was based on standardized tests which were objective and valid. As a result, for decades blacks accepted the decisions of these so called "objective tests" as a plethora of academic and vocational development options were eliminated for generations of black children due to the negative consequences of these tests. However, in the wake of the Civil Rights movement and some significant movement toward school desegregation, more black parents, teachers, and other black educational professionals, began to take a closer look at the issues of standardized testing. As a result, they began to challenge the objectivity and even the very validity of these tests which, for so long, had been used to determine the educational future, and consequently, economic opportunities for black children. They began to analyze the structure, various components, and presentation of these tests. As a result, they determined that these sacrosanct tests were, for the most part, irrational, arbitrary, and invalid with regards to measuring or predicting the capacity and capabilities of black children. Why, because the control or norm groups for these vaunted standardized tests were constructed based, exclusively, on samples of white middle class children. It was quite obvious, that these white middle class children possessed a body of information as a result of their particular life experiences that was all but totally alien to low-income black children.

Legal challenges to the use of these tests for decision making in schools have focused in the areas of ability tracking, special education placement, admission criteria, and teacher competency. Many court cases have been based on the claim that these kinds of standardized test have caused a disproportionate number of blacks and other none white minorities to be placed in low ability tracks. These arguments have been predicated on the substantiated evidence that these standardized tests were biased against the lowest scoring groups, and are only reflecting the results of past segregation in the schools. The plaintiffs have argued that these tests have denied them the access to certain educational programs or certification of some kind. In some cases, the courts have upheld these arguments and sought to remedy this pervasive problem.

In the case of, Hobson verses Hansen in 1967, the court held that the I.Q. test used to track students were culturally bias because they were standardized on a white middle class sample. The court ruled that these tests were inaccurate for lower class none whites and black students. As a result, the court subsequently abolished the tracking system used in the District of Columbia. Although further appeals on the part of district officials, did allow for some type of ability grouping, however, the schools were no longer allowed to use the standardized tests, with their racially discriminatory consequences.

Many blacks found that the use of the Achievement Test was just as inappropriate as the I.Q. Test for making decisions regarding the educational placement of their children. The case of, Moses verses the Washington Parish School Board in 1971 involved the use of the I.Q. and the Achievement test. The I.Q. test was used for special education placement, and the

Achievement test scores were used for later tracking. The court ruled against the use of both tests. This case was unique, because it involved a recently desegregated school district.

Perhaps the best-known test case was concerned with special education placement. The case of, *Larry T. vs. Riles* in 1972 involved the use of I.Q. Tests to place students in E.M.R. class "Educable Mentally Retarded." The school district argued that test's results were not the sole bases for the racial imbalance of blacks in E.M.R. classes, since parental consent was required. However, the court decided that test's scores were also influencing parents. Therefore, the court was not sympathetic to the district's position. In later appeals, test's validity became the main focus and the court set standards for validity. It declared that the same pattern of scores must appear in different sub-groups. It further insisted that the mean score should be the same for different sub-groups, and the results should correlate with relevant criterion measures. Linguistics biases have been another bases upon which these tests have been challenged. In Diana verses California State Board of Education in 1970, the court ruled that Mexican Americans must be given the test in Spanish. This resulted in these students gaining an additional fourteen points as a result of the removal of this language bias. The court rule that any standardized scores must be substantiated through an evaluation of the student's developmental history, cultural background, and academic achievement.

In a landmark decision, a three-judge panel of the Ninth District upheld a lower court's prohibition of the use of the I.Q. Test because it was culturally biased against blacks. As a result, it could no longer be use for the placement of black children in special education classes. However, this court decision only affects those states in the Northwest area of the nation. So with the nationwide attention on standardized tests for educational guidance, there is little doubt that there will be any significant nation-wide change without more court action. The Stanford Nine and the Wechsler Intelligence Scale for children, two of the most widely use testing instruments in the nation, were incidentally, band in California and most of the Pacific Northwest as sole instruments in the consideration of student placement.

David Lethbridge in his review of the *Bell Curve* by Richard Herstein and Charles Murray asserts that the book is nothing more than just pseudo-scientific racist propaganda. He further points out that Herstein, who is a faculty member of Harvard University, is nothing more than an apologist for racial inequality and class oppression. Herstein and Murray's book is replete with references from a collection of racists Nazis and anti-Semites, who are far more interested in advancing their own racist agendas than in any legitimate scientific inquiry. Many of these so-called scientific authorities, of which Herstein has based his argument of black innate inferiority to whites, are connected with a journal name, *"Mankind Quarterly"*. The founder and editor of this journal, Robert Gayre, championed South Africa's Apartheid and have often stated his asinine belief that blacks are worthless. Henry Garrett is another rabid racist and anti-Semite, who belongs to the

White Citizen's Counsel. Corraco Jini, a leading biologist in Mussolini's Italy and author of the Scientific Bases for Fascism, is another one of these so-called authorities cited in the *Bell Curve*. Also, Ottmar Von Verschuer, is a devotee of Josef Mengele, the fiendish monster of Nazi Germany who perpetrated such heinous atrocities against death camp prisoners, that his sadistic deeds still challenge every known definition of sanity. Even more significantly, Robert Person who has been connected with "Mankind Quarterly" for the past twenty-five years was the leader of a pro-Fascist group named the Northern League. This organization was composed primarily of former Nazi officials and other white supremacist.

Murray and Herstien are quick to acknowledge their guidance and reliance on the literature of Richard Lyn, a professor of Psychology in Northern Ireland. Lyn is also an associate editor of "Mankind Quarterly. His work is cited in the "Bell Curve", no less than twenty four times. Murray and Herstein notes Lyn assertion that the I.Q. of blacks in Africa is only 70, given a statistical average of 100 as an abstract universal benchmark. Although, Lyn maintains that 70, is a valid approximation of black I.Q. capacity throughout Africa, it is based on a single survey conducted in 1989. This survey was conducted with 1,000 sixteen-year-olds, using the South African Junior aptitude test. Furthermore, the actual author of the study was not Lyn, but Dr. Ken Owen. Owen suggests that the results of the test, in no way, insinuated the biological inferiority of blacks, but reflected the poor quality of black education under apartheid.

Nevertheless, Lyn, Herstein, and Murray still insist upon drawing racist implications, not only with Owen's study, but many others conducted under apartheid. Why, because they are obviously consumed with a perversely ethnocentric need to validate their scurvy notion of white skinned biological superiority over none whites.

Consequently, it is inevitably predictable that such vicious and unmitigatedly racist ideologue like Lyn, Herstein, and Murray are totally committed to attributing every difference between blacks and whites to some kind of warped notion of white skinned biological superiority. Therefore, one should not be surprised at the focus, tone, methodology, and obviously, specious conclusions of their so called research. Moreover, they are further implicated by the philosophies of those organizations which are the primary sources of their funding. The "Mankind Quarterly" is funded primarily by the Pioneer Fund. This is an organization founded in 1937 by American millionaire, Wickliffe Draper and others who were staunch supporters of Nazi Germany. Since its inception, the Pioneer Fund has aligned itself and been an avid supporter of virtually every white supremacist group in America and around the world. This fund has given financial support to such racist psychologist like Arthur Jensen and Philipe Rushton, both who claim that blacks are biologically inferior to whites. Also, it has given financial support to William Shockley, inventor of the transistor, and who also made the despicable statement that blacks should be paid not to reproduce, because their progeny would only further destroy the national gene pool.

220

Also, the Pioneer Fund has given its financial support to such groups as the Foundation of Human Understanding. This same Foundation of Human Understanding distributed copies of Herstein and Jensen's work to colleges and universities throughout the nation during the 1970's, in an attempt to influence them not to admit blacks. Just as the American Immigration Control Federation, the *Bell Curve* makes its assertions of white biological superiority from its own body of unscientific information and tries to pass these specious claims off as valid, reliable, and legitimate science. Murray and Herstein contends that because the average intelligence of none white, Third World people, is far less than whites, the continued immigration of these none whites is putting downward pressure on America's distribution of intelligence. So this is the insidious, diabolical, and coldly calculated effort on the part of white supremacists who operate unabated around the globe.

This pseudo-scientific dogma of white skinned biological superiority over all other people, classified as nonwhite, is the lynch pen of this world-wide system of economic exploitation and political oppression created to dehumanize, inferiorize, and marginalize them. Its primary objective for blacks in this nation as well as those on the African continent is, to keep them thoroughly miseducated, intellectually dysfunctional, economically Impotent, and politically irrelevant. Consequently, they remained locked in a racial cast: subsisting by and large, as a poverty stricken, powerless, and dependent group. This well orchestrated, highly routinized, and meticulously managed racial cast system was created, implemented, and maintained by the most intelligent collective of white people on the planet. Their conscious effort to reserve such a superordinate political an economic position for themselves, and an unmitigatedly subordinate or inferior status for blacks is frightening when one considers the global scale upon which it has been organized and is functioning. However, what is even more frightening, is that, many of even the most intelligent of us blacks, haven't the vaguest idea of how to properly identify white supremacy as a deeply entrenched world-wide political and economic structure, or analyze it in the context of its global implications on the survival of none white people. Furthermore, with all of our miseducation and training in the arts and sciences of our masters, most of our so called scholars, are simply bereft of the legitimate rational, critical, or analytical skills to construct some kind of black political, economic, or psychological behavioral model that could halt, or perhaps reverse the devastating effects of white supremacy on none white people.

Finally, the pitiful condition of our status as a people in America and around the world should automatically impose every moral, intellectual, and scientific imperative on the best and brightest of us to find an answer to our dilemma. That answer should first yield a reprieve, and then total liberation from our oppression at the hands of the global white oligarchy which administers this political and economic system of white supremacy: created and maintained only to exploit and oppress none white peoples in general, and black people in particular. However, this laudable objective can never be achieved unless or until, we black folk, truly endeavor to understand what really happened to our minds and souls during that four and a half centuries experience of chattel slavery and finally accept the hideous truth about our tragic history in America. Then we must equip ourselves, through the process of true, self-directed education, with the critical and analytical skills to think rationally, behave responsibly, and deal effectively with our environment. This is the kind of realistic, critical, and analytical approach to problem solving, that will compel our intelligentsia to finally create a rational psychological paradigm and workable cultural model that will enable us to confirm our humanity, acknowledge our unique ethnicity, and reclaim control of the politics and economy of our community. Furthermore, this kind of intelligent and scientific approach to our problem, will finally enable us to reclaim our cultural sanity and start adopting attitudes and behavior patterns that will serve the economic and political interest of our own group, just like other nations.

We must come to grips with the unassailable fact that, America, is nothing but a nation of ethnic nations. Every white as well as honorary white ethnic group in America has achieved economic control over their respective communities and a measure of political power in this society, by organizing and mobilizing themselves around their own unique ethnic identity and group interests. So in a nation of various ethnic nations, it is only we black Americans, who continue to be trained to behave as a group of disorganized, dysfunctional, and totally Impotent individuals, especially when measured against the overwhelming collective economic and political might of the various ethnic nations in this country. This is why it is so easy for these honorary-white, Middle-Eastern, Asian, and other Immigrants to continue the economic rape of our community and then dominate our economy. These honorary-white aliens systematically drain the wealth from our community, all be it, with our own pathetically unwise and tragically misguided cooperation and support by spending all of our money with them, making it more and more Impoverished, while steadily enriching their own. Ironically, they come right into our community exhibiting the same old racist attitudes and demonstrating the same brazen contempt for us, as do most whites.

Moreover, due to their stereotypical attitudes and racist beliefs about blacks that they have acquired from their white benefactors these ethnics staunchly refuse to live in our community, where they amass their fortunes. Also, they consistently refuse to spend any of their own money, whatsoever with us. However, every time a black man or woman points out this stupendously deleterious trade imbalance, these same self-serving racists hypocrites invariably attack him or her as being unreasonable and ethnically intolerant, when their own duplicitous behavior is the very epitome of ethnic intolerance. These racist petty-bourgeois parasites even have the litigated gall to pompously assert that they should have the right and freedom, to locate their businesses in our community and drain off the wealth: while simultaneously frantically resisting any prospect of allowing black businesses to exist in their own closed communities.

However, even if a black man or woman were successful in locating a business in one of these ethnic communities, these honorary white residents would certainly refuse, as a group, to patronize it. Why, this is undoubtedly because, the primary requirement for achieving and maintaining their honorary-white social and political status in America, is to constantly prove to the genuine white folk, that they are maintaining their indelibly racist attitudes toward, and utter contempt for blacks in every conceivable area of human behavior. These people use their common cultural experiences to behave as a nation to dominate the economy of our community and ruthlessly exploit us. This is why they always manage to rest control of the economic life of our community, because we yet insist on behaving like a group of disorganized, dysfunctional, and disconnected individuals.

Therefore, logic dictates that we black Americans finally recognize and appreciate the wisdom of this time-tested ethnic group mobilization strategy for gaining economic and political control over our own community. Consequently, the most logical and intelligent alternative to our economic, social, and political problems in America is a serious and rapid move toward a rational and emphatic ethnic and cultural identity and true African nationhood. Furthermore, we must totally embrace our own unique ethnic values and systematically practice the most basic and common sense adage of putting the political and economic interests of our own group first.

In other words, we must resolve to seriously restructure our economic and political behavior so as to accomplish everything that this idea of African-American nationhood implies and in deed requires. So when the relentless pressures of economic deprivation and political powerlessness will have, at last, forced us to finally abandoned our slavish devotion to, and intellectually absurd obsession with this absurd idea and baseless notion of rugged individualism, then perhaps we will finally embrace the economic imperative to come together as a bona fide African nation. Then we will at last have the political and economic ability to effectively utilize our group strength, in the same ways that other ethnic groups have been doing to improve the political and economic status of their entire groups, for generations in America. Then, and only then, we will have the power to set national goals and priorities for liberating ourselves from the deleterious effects of institutional racism, or white supremacy.

CHAPTER 14

Taking Back Our African Mind

So often I've heard far too many African-Americans complain about studying their history. Their objections range from the sublime to the ridiculous: " ... """That stuff is in the past." ... "It's nothing but a waste of time." ... "So what, if Africans built the great pyramids, what are they doing now?" ... "What about all the ancient African kings and queens, and their fantastic deeds, how's that going to help me now?"" The American educational system has expertly taught, in fact trained African-Americans to view Africa and African peoples, not only as insignificant in world history who have made no significant contribution to human civilization, but also that the African continent is totally irrelevant to our experience here in America. We have been systematically trained or indoctrinated to view Africa and her peoples only through the eyes of White Western European culture. As a result, the great majority of us regard Africa and her various native peoples as primitive, backwards, and unable to govern themselves or exploit their natural resources. Consequently, most of us, not only feel no genuine familial kinship for Africa or her peoples, but show the same condescension or thinly veiled Ethnocentric contempt as most Whites do: the fact that we African-Americans are inextricably physically and culturally tied to that continent not withstanding. This is the result of having our minds systematically programmed and our strongest attitudes, basic values, and deepest beliefs about ourselves and the rest of the world profoundly shaped by the conscious and unconscious forces of White Western European culture.

African-Americans are, for all intents and purposes, black skinned people with a White Western European mentality which shapes, dictates, and colors all of our conscious as well as unconscious behavior. This tragic mass brainwashing was accomplished during our four and a half centuries of chattel slavery. Our African ancestors were torn from their native land, packed like cordwood in the hulls of sailing ships, and hauled across the Atlantic Ocean, never to see their homeland again. When they arrived in the western hemisphere, they were distributed throughout North and South America and the Caribbean Islands to be sold like horses, cattle, sheep, and hogs. However, in order to perpetrate this inexpiable evil against Africans,

The European power elite along with their American counterparts decided to arbitrarily defined all black skinned peoples as primordial beast with no souls, ape-like minds, and innately inferior to themselves. This pathetically arbitrary and totally capricious definition of the African and his kind was done so that the White Western European elite could ruthlessly subjugate and exploit them without any restriction of morality or restraint of conscious. As a result of this damnable moral and ethical relegation of the African from human to beast, these White Western

228

European elites set about concocting and perpetuating all manner of myths, stereotypes and pseudo-scientific dogma suggesting black skinned innate inferiority to whites in order to justify their bottomless barbarity against them. Therefore, they regarded these African captives as naturally inferior to themselves. They even redefined these Africans as a species of primitive, primeval, sub-human; ape-like creatures whose strong backs, limited intelligence, and native physical endurance made them perfect candidates for the cultivation and economic exploitation of their plantation-based economies in the "New World". Consequently these Europeans imposed upon them, the legal status of personal property. As a result, these Africans were stripped of every vestige of their humanity and reduced to pieces of personal property, to be bought and sold like horses, mules, oxen, and other beasts of burden.

This meant that Western European law defined the African as a commodity, a piece of commercial property or product to be bought and sold in the marketplaces of the world. As a result, for more than four centuries, these African captives were bought and sold in commercial centers throughout the world, just like other common livestock, agricultural goods, and manufactured products. Ironically, their "Christian" masters were released from all natural constraints of morality as well as all other convictions of human conscious concerning their treatment of the African, because they defined and regarded him as merely a piece of property. So how could these white "Christians" possibly be held to any moral or ethical account for the way they handled their personal property? Those

Europeans, who operated the trans-Atlantic slave trade, totally stripped the African slave of his humanity. In other words, they systematically stripped the African captive of every vestige of his native culture: his language, religion, values, beliefs, customs, and traditions which had made him what and who he had been for generations in Africa. As a result, he was transformed from a spiritually and psychologically whole, free-thinking human being, with a viable and intact history and a culture, into a thing: a Negro.

The Negro was the original, hideous and pathetically tragic, Frankenstein monster. His mind was wiped clean of everything that he originally was and had been in his native land, and then reprogrammed with everything that he was not under the total domination and systematic indoctrination of chattel slavery. His memory was not only wiped clean of Africa and his native African culture, moreover, he was taught to despise, revile, and even hate everything black or African. In other words, he was consistently taught to despise, reject, and revile his natural and normal black African self and his kind. Conversely, he was trained and conditioned to love, prize, and pine for everything that was white and European. This systematic brainwashing of the Negro lasted for more than twenty-two generations, and even continues to cripple and distort his mind today. As a result, this relentless racial brainwashing imposed on the Negro's mind, afflicted him with a mentally crippling and virtually terminal schizophrenia from which he has yet to recover. Any honest examination of the institution of chattel slavery in Western European culture, will reveal that the Negro was created under an unspeakably wicket system of physical brutality and psychological subjugation that would shock even the most sadistic mind. He was systematically terrorized, vilified, and brutalized with every conceivable means of physical and psychological torture that could be concocted by the twisted mind of his ruthlessly fiendish and egomaniacal masters. In other words, he was terrorized, traumatized, disfigured, mutilated, and murdered into total physical and psychological submission to his omnipotent white master. Having been subjected to four and a half centuries of a kind of bottomless brutality, that has never been equaled in the annals of human history, the Negro has had imposed upon him, a morbid and all consuming fear of white folk.

Moreover, this deep-seated terror of white skinned people is indelible and has been effectively transmitted from one generation to the next. While the Negro has been trained to be ever terrified of, and unquestioningly obedient to, his white master, he has simultaneously been conditioned to love, worship, deify, and idealize his master's vaunted culture. Ironically, any natural hatred the Negro has for his master, as a result of his master's ruthless savagery against him, has been internalized and turned against his own kind. In other words, the natural hatred for the white master as a result of his sadistic brutality against the Negro, he channels toward other Negroes.

Consequently, that which the Negro has already been trained to hate and revile becomes the natural object of his pent up rage and mindless violence. Therefore, since the Negro has been forced fed for four and a half centuries on a steady diet of total self-hatred and total detestation for Africa and his kind, there is little wonder why we lead the nation in every category of crimes against each other. However, and even sadder commentary is, that since so called integration and the post-Civil Rights era, the social pathologies of mindless violence, drug abuse, and family disintegration have actually accelerated: statistics show that two-thirds of African-American households are headed by single females. Moreover, statistics have reveal that nearly half of the federal prison population is African-American and that an alarming number of young black males are either incarcerated or on parole. Now combined these sorry statistics with incredibly poor education, the rate of black high school dropout, and the critical level of perpetually high black unemployment and under employment, then the pathetic poverty and shameful social disorganization of our community becomes clear and predictable.

Now, why should we study our history? Because it is the only discipline that holds the key to freeing us from the mass insanity that has been inflicted upon us for more than twenty-two generations of being forced to exist as white folk personal property: in effect, their beasts of burden. Although, we were supposedly freed after the Civil War ended in 1865, we were still relegated to a racial cast in this nation imposed by a legal system of racial apartheid for another one hundred years. Consequently, we were forced to languish for decades at the very bottom of this economy while we watched other non-black immigrants come to this nation from every corner of the globe and freely take advantage o social and economic opportunities that had been denied us for generations, simply because of our her

232

itage and skin color. We were forced to endure a sorry subsistence plight as second-class citizens under a legally sanctioned apartheid in this nation. Under this scurvy system of racial domination and control of the entire black population, only we African-Americans were denied those basic human and political rights that all other Americans enjoyed as a matter of their citizenship.

For example, only Negroes because of our race and heritage were denied the following civil rights and privileges: the right to vote, serve on juries, work in certain public jobs, eat in certain restaurants, stay in certain hotels, use certain hospitals, patronize public libraries, attend many public schools, colleges, and universities, and set wherever we pleased on public buses, trains, and other forms of public transportation. Moreover, we were also denied the citizenship right to purchase homes in certain areas of cities and towns throughout this country because of our heritage and skin color. Furthermore, the white elite even took the very idea of black race and heritage to a ridiculously absurd extreme. They decreed that any individual possessing even one drop of African blood was considered to be a Negro. This whole perverse notion was only a legal effort to control and circumscribe the social, political, and especially economic behavior of the white master's slave offspring. In other words, to make certain that they could not legally marry other whites, inherit property or any other form of wealth from their white masters, or have real access to any of the other civil rights and privileges that other non-black Americans enjoyed as a matter of their American citizenship.

Although much of this slave progeny, was the spitting image of its white masters, due to the fact that one of the parents had been a slave, the children were automatically defined as black and Negro and consequently relegated to that designated racial cast reserved for blacks. In 1892 Homer Adolph Plessy, an African-American shoemaker from New Orleans, Louisiana, was arrested for sitting in a, "Whites Only", section of a railroad car. Judge John Ferguson found him guilty of the crime of refusing to leave the "Whites Only" section of the railroad car. Plessy subsequently appealed to both Supreme Courts of Louisiana and the United States, however both court's upheld Ferguson's previous decision and the "Separate but Equal" doctrine became a legal fact of United States law. So the "Plessy VS Ferguson" decision became a legally sanctioned racial apartheid in American law and life in 1896. Homer Adolph Plessy had been a very light-skinned man with obvious white physical features. However, several white passengers head recognized him as having Negro heritage and had subsequently reported this to the train conductor. So Homer Plessy's only problem was, that he'd been accused of having at least one drop of Negro blood and had had the unmitigated audacity to set in the "Whites Only" section of a railroad car. It is simply an unspeakable travesty of even a pretense of justice that this guilty nation and its fellow culprits of Europe have never even considered the proposition of giving us, the direct descendants of their countless victims, anything in the way of economic or material compensation for four hundred and fifty years of free labor and unspeakable human suffering and psychological degradation.

Furthermore, to this day, this government, along with the rest of those guilty nations of Europe, that perpetrated this unspeakably horrific human holocaust against us, refuses to even consider any form of compensation or reparations, for the four and a half centuries of savage barbarity that they perpetrated against our people. Ironically, these same governments have compensated other people that they have damaged: the Jews, the Japanese, and to some degree, Native Americans. America's Marshall Plan of economic aid, literally rebuilt Europe and Japan after the mass destruction of World War II. However, whenever the question of reparations comes up concerning the four and a half century holocaust against African-Americans, there is a deafening and despicable silence. What is even worst, there are some very vociferous, self-serving, sycophantic, and unspeakably pathetic house Negroes who are always rushing forward trying to defend the American government's rationally indefensible, and morally reprehensible position to remain silent in the wake of its culpability concerning its role in the African holocaust. So the whole white world continues to stand pathetically mute in its unfathomable pretense of innocence on the issue of reparations for their barbarous crimes against black skinned people for more than four centuries.

What is even more scandalous, is that too many of us African-Americans, the direct descendants of those tragic victims, have been intimidated by whites, or simply shamed into a cowardly silence by those vociferous self-serving bourgeois house Negroes among us, while the voices of our ancestors cry out from their graves, for justice and redress of this cataclysmic

235

crime. So the voices of countless millions of black skinned human beings, who were force to live all the days of their natural lives, as white folk personal property, continue to cry out from their graves in their righteous indignation, for us, the living, to stand up and demand justice, which is nothing less than appropriate compensation and reparations from America and the other guilty nations of Europe. Moreover, every dictate of conscience and morality requires that we demands this kind of unadulterated justice, for the millions of victims of the absolute worse crime against humanity, ever recorded in the annals of world history. Therefore, every precept of morality and ethicality as well as every valid concept of justice, known to civilized man, demands restitution from these culprits who perpetrated this demoniacal holocaust against an entire group of people, which lasted for more than four centuries, with skin color and geography as the only criteria for victimization. Even after the close of the Civil War, it took another one hundred years of protest and several U.S. Supreme Court decisions before we could finally enjoy the same basic rights of citizenship that white Americans took for granted.

Furthermore, during the nearly one hundred years after the Civil War ended, we were literally locked out of the general economy of this nation. So when I hear black people pining nostalgically about how we use to own all kinds of businesses and how we use to trade with each other, I have to frown and shake my head. Yes, we certainly did, own all kinds of businesses, and we indeed regularly traded with each other too. Why? Because white folk insisted that we stay in our place

236

(a nigger's place) and they wouldn't allow us to patronize their businesses, that's why? Now that we have "integrated", more accurately, disintegrated as a viable community, we've all but given up our separate economy. As a result, now we're all the worst off for it too. So we spent the better part of two decades protesting, marching, and praying until we finally won the right to give our money to white business men and women, whom had previously rejected it, because they rejected us. However, it made us feel so good to have the legal right to spend our money with people whom had historically rejected and despised us, to the point that they didn't even want our money; we just totally turned our backs on our own businessmen and women. We were so caught up in the rapturous spirit of integration that we totally dismissed the fact that our black businessmen and women were the primary creators of jobs in our community. This crucial fact not withstanding, we still gleefully turned our backs on them. Now what was this all for, to give our money to a hostile white population with the same historically racist view of us as sub-human and innately inferior to themselves, just as they had had before, "Integration".

What the Negro has tragically failed to understand, is the fact that the same racist mentality that enable some white folk to dehumanize and turn black skinned people into beasts of burden and commercial property, and for those not directly involved with the institutional of chattel slavery, to quiescently accept and even embrace this damnable crime, is fluid, and is still being inexorably transmitted from one generation to the next. Since its inception, this indelible myth of innate black skinned inferiority and innate white skinned superiority has been stamped on the consciousness of every generation of white, as well as black skinned people born and raised in white western European culture. This is poignant and irrefutable evidence as to why there will never be any genuine acceptance of Negroes as social equals on the part of the great majority of white people in this nation.

Furthermore, nor will the white power elite of this nation, or any nation that they control, ever allow the Negro to share in any meaningful exercise of political or economic power. The mere proposition of the Negro actually exercising any significant independent economic or political power is simply a logical impossibility, especially not to any extent where, such an exercise of this power would threaten to significantly alter the historically oppressive and exploitative relationship between the two groups. So again, why study our history? If the Negro is ever going to rise above his self-destructive behavior as a Frankenstein monster, created only to serve the selfish interest of his fiendish master, he must turn to the heeling powers which can only come from a true knowledge of his own history. I do not mean just the story of his pathetically tragic sojourn throughout the Caribbean and in the Americas, but his true African history which dates back thousands of years before the rise of Western Europe.

The educational institutions created and maintained by White Western European culture cannot and will never teach the Negro the unadulterated truth about himself. Why? Because they would have to simultaneously reveal the horrific and profoundly putrescent truth about white people too. However, this is a very frightening proposition that the great majority of white folk are not willing to entertain. Why? Because they realize that in order to teach the Negro the objective truth about himself, this proposition would invariably compel them to have to tell the whole scandalous truth about themselves too. Therefore, they cannot possibly, teach the objective story of the Negro or African, without also revealing their own unmitigatedly savage and barbaric role in that same experience. These Europeans would be obliged to admit that they arbitrarily and unilaterally relegated fellow human beings to the legal status of personal property, forced them to live as beast of burden, and used them as commodities to be bought and sold. Furthermore, they would have to explain the insatiable greed and bottomless depravity within themselves that could allow them to totally and so thoroughly divorce themselves from every principle and precept of morality, rationality, and ethicality known to human civilization, in order to perpetrate such an unspeakably heinous crime on fellow human beings for four and a half centuries.

Of course, the great majority of white folk are in no way, willing to expose themselves to the prospect of possessing such an unfathomably malevolent and malignant collective character defect. Conversely, they would rather consistently insist on taking flight into fantasy, which amounts to a staunch denial of any culpability for such a heinous crime against humanity. They tenaciously cling to the perverse notion that the trans-Atlantic slave trade, was actually for the poor African's own good. After all, didn't they bring him out of hopeless superstition and primitive savagery in Africa and introduce him to White Western European Culture, thereby civilizing and Christianizing him? However, they always fail to concede the fact that the countless millions of captives, torn from their homes in Africa, for more than four centuries, actually never had any voice or choice in the matter. Furthermore, they will never concede the glaring fact that these conscienceless traffickers in human flesh, were never, in the least, concern with the African's cultural, or any other form of development, they were only interested in exploiting him as an economic tool, because they were actually motivated by their own lust for power and insatiable greed for wealth and material comfort. So for more than four centuries, America and nearly every nation of Europe, looked toward Africa for their endless supply of black bodies as the answer to their accumulation of wealth: the total destruction of a whole continent of people was only an incidental means to their economic ends. So, white folk can only but continue their hopelessly pathetic denial of their diabolical role in creating Negroes. Why? Because if they ever mustered enough courage and honesty to face the naked truth, it will invariably expose them as an infinitely more hideous species of monster than the one that they created.

Consequently, White Western European institutions will never seriously endeavor to teach the truth about history, their own, or the African's. For if the White Western European mind ever rationally concedes that the African is a fellow human being, then because of its savagely sadistic barbarity against him, it cannot escape the logical conclusion that it is totally and completely insane, by every rational and valid definition of the term. Moreover, when one examines the cultural matrix that had the capacity to produce such a mind capable of perpetrating such sadistic physical brutality and unconscionable psychological malevolence against fellow human beings, then the inescapable conclusion reveals that such a culture is the very epitome of narcissism, hypocrisy, and moral degeneracy. This is the primary rational and ethical principle that White Western Europeans are afraid of, and this is why the great majority of them will not, and cannot ever tell the whole truth about their own history, or that of any other non-white skinned people whom they have destroyed in order to feed their unquenchable lust for power and wealth. They know that they are guilty of perpetrating a crime against a whole continent of people that shocks every dictate of sanity and civilization. Furthermore, what is even more damnable was that the only requirement for the African's unspeakable victimization was skin color and geographical origin.

Although the White Western European elite certainly realizes that the enormous scale of its heinous brutality and bottomless barbarity against African peoples is without parallel in the annals of world history, it has been determined to absorb itself of any recrimination based upon its own perverse myth, superstition, and pseudo-scientific dogma regarding the African's innate inferiority. Therefore, these white folk have never been ashamed or guilty enough to make restitution for their fiendish and diabolical four and a half centuries holocaust against African peoples. Why, because they still choose to cling to the notion that they have committed no crime, after all, chattel slavery also benefited the African, didn't it? Why hadn't it rescued him from his primitive savagery on a hopelessly backwards continent and raised him to an acceptable level of "civilized Christian living"? This observation only poignantly underscores the glaring fact that the same deprave mythology of black skinned inferiority and white skinned superiority is yet alive and well in the White Western European consciousness. Consequently, it remains fluid and still saturates every conceivable aspect of Western European culture and continues to be transmitted, in its totality, from one generation to the next. This is the nature of the mass insanity which afflicts the Western European mind.

This mass pathology is the malignant malevolence which invariably shapes all Western European basic attitudes, values, and beliefs and as a result dictates all conscious and unconscious thought and behavior toward all people whom have been classified as nonwhite on this planet. As I have fore stated, White Western European culture is not only the all powerful and all pervasive force that shapes basic attitudes and values for whites toward blacks, but it also fundamentally shapes basic black attitudes, values, and belief toward whites and also toward blacks themselves. Consequently, when one takes a closer look at the racists dogma which emanates from the very matrix of Western European culture, then the unimpeachable evidence of the myth of white skinned innate superiority and black skinned innate inferiority is clearly

242

present, pervasive, and extremely potent. Moreover, White Western European racist dogma has assigned a complete body or pattern of appropriate behavior to each designated group: the innately inferior blacks and the innately superior whites.

For example, those who are classified as white or superior, are taught from the cradle to the grave that they are the most fit and are divinely anointed to occupy the superior position concerning all things of significance on the planet. Conversely, those who have been classified as black or inferior are taught by this culture, that they have been divinely cursed and are therefore relegated to occupy the bottom or inferior position in all significant areas of human life and experience. Moreover, the systematic reinforcement of these two distinct and clearly recognizable patterns of behavior regarding both groups, are ever present, pervasive, and potent in every conceivable aspect of human life. For example, our whole prescription for social existence is constantly demonstrated and reinforced by every institution in this society: the family, church, school, and the print and electric medias. Therefore we are systematically reminded and constantly reinforced with the powerful message during every minute of our conscious lives, precisely where are superior or inferior place is, and exactly how to stay in it.

We all remember the black Psychologists Kenneth Clark and his famous doll test, which was presented as compelling and powerful psychological evidence showing the tragically self-destructive impact of racial attitudes on black children during the "Brown vs the Board of Education of Topeka, Kansas" trial concerning the issue of public school integration for black children. This famous case was finally settled by a unanimous U.S. Supreme Court verdict in 1954. In brief, Doctor Clark presented a number of black children with a choice of two dolls, one white and the other black. Then he asked each child a number of questions about the two dolls, for example, which doll is the smartest? Which one is the prettiest? Which doll represents you? Which doll represents the kind of person that you wish to be or wish that you were? Almost without exception, the black children chose the white doll. Doctor Clark's test reveal to those white Supreme Court Justices only what most of us already knew, because we too have been subjected to that same insidious insanity, that black children were being thoroughly and profoundly programmed to hate themselves while loving and desiring to be white people. So there is little wonder, that far too many of us African-Americans, in our secret hearts, still actually prefer to date and mate with white folk, or at least those lighter skinned members of our own group: those who are definitely closer in appearance to Europeans. Why, because even today, the European physical profile is our quintessential standard and ultimate ideal of physical beauty and sex appeal.

Consequently, the great majority of us African-American men and women still desperately pine and fantasizing our secret harts to date and mate with white folk in our vain attempt to bask in the ethereal glow of their omnipotent Western European whiteness. Conversely, yet the great majority of us, in our secret heart of hearts, desperately dread, totally detest, and absolutely abhor the very idea of having

244

to date, mate or even having to deal with our own kind. However, the root of our pathetically tragic mental illness stems from our four and a half centuries of total white domination and systematic racial indoctrination, which has made us scandalously intellectually dishonest, psychologically dysfunctional, and spiritually dead.

Therefore, African-Americans must realize that the study of our history as well as our oppressor's history will be our own responsibility. We will also learn from an honest examination of African history, that the black man and woman, is the Father and mother of this planet. We will further learn that all human progress and development began in, and then moved out from Africa, even man himself, began there. It is an unassailable fact that every concept, precept, principle, and idea of culture and human civilization originated from the black man and woman in Africa. The only real hope for the Negro to finally free himself from his psychologically crippling self-hatred and reclaim his natural African mind and consequently, his own humanity, lies in the study of his own rich and spiritually empowering history. There he will find his true African identity, his rightful place in his community, and his divine purpose on this planet. I've often heard conscious and rationally thinking African-Americans say, "If a man don't treat you right, why do you think he'll teach you right?" The Negro, and the Negro mentality of a loving, fawning, obsequious obsession to be exactly like white folk, only serves the selfish interest of white folk. How? Because they know that a Negro's only real ambition in life is to be a facsimile of his master. He wants to live as near white folk as they will allow him, spend all of his money with white folk, and mimic the attitudes, appearance, and behavior of white folk.

The most wealthy and successful Negroes in America are the group observed as, W. E. B. Dubois's so called, "talented tenth": although E. Franklin Frazier refers to this group as the "Black Bourgeoisie". However, despite their income, education, or training, they will never invest their time or their money in the development of the black community. Why? Because they have been expertly trained and conditioned, through their indoctrination by America's educational institutions, to thoroughly and completely hate themselves and their kind. Therefore, their primary goal in life, after, (having made it), is to get the hell away, and stay as far away from other less fortunate blacks as they possibly can. Consequently, these obsequious preening and prancing Negro elites are thoroughly imbued with the same condescending and contemptuous attitudes and behavior toward other African-Americans as most overtly racist whites. They are far too busy trying to mimic the attitudes and effect the bourgeois trappings of petty self-indulgence and conspicuous consumption as their white peers. So again, only a sincere and in depth study of African history is the medicine that has the real power to remedy our psychologically crippling schizophrenia which is the primary source of our mass insanity. This kind of honest and systematic study of our history also offers the only genuine hope for reclaiming our rightful African mind. I am convinced that through this kind of serious and systematic study of our true history, we can finally re-connect with our

246

true culture, our true selves, and our true God. When we are able to spiritually re-connect with our true African God, then we can allow his Divine Spirit, living in us, to rise up and empower us to finally liberate our minds and bodies. When we achieve this, we will have thrown off the mental chains of white indoctrination and economic exploitation and finally be free as self-directed and psychologically whole human beings.

CHAPTER 15

The Black Clergy's Response to the Million-Man March

The white press decried it, white politicians despised it, and most of the so- called black leaders discouraged it. Still it happened. On October 16, 1995, African-American men made history when nearly two million of us gathered at the capital in Washington D.C. I was there, and I witnessed a rare spiritual ambiance of love, peace and unity among African-American men that will be indelibly imprinted on my heart and mind. I observed for the first time in my life multitudes of black men showing genuine affection and brotherhood toward each other. I witnessed them by the hundreds and thousands, laughing together, crying together and showing the kind of honest heart felt emotion that even they, had actually forgotten they were capable of expressing. I embraced, shook hands with, and laughed and cried with black men from all over this land who had come to the nation's capital to reclaim their lost humanity and assert their self- respect through spiritual atonement.

The platform featured a host of eloquent speakers who exalted, inspired and encouraged us to raise our children, love and respect our women, and provide for and protect our families. They exhorted us to be real men. The platform featured such notables as Dorothy Height, Maya Angelou, and Dr. Betty

248

Shabazz, the widow of the late Malcolm X, Mayor Marion Berry, Rev. Jesse Jackson and a number of others who spoke the unadulterated truth with such passionate fervor that they pulled on our heartstrings and stirred our souls. We were moved to the point that we were often in tears as we testified to their words like a great church congregation.

The massive crowd was electrified with a kind of positive display of genuine affection and sober reflection that I have never witnessed among black people anywhere, at any time in my life. The crowd was polite, cordial and most receptive to all of the speakers. However, as the day wore on, it was obvious whom these men had really come to hear. As the bright October sun reached its apex and began to descend toward the western horizon, the rhythmic chant of, "Farrakhan, Farrakhan, Farrakhan", would course through the massive crowd of black bodies, which stretched from the capital building and beyond the Washington Monument. The combined voices of nearly two million black men chanting "Farrakhan, Farrakhan, Farrakhan", sounded like mighty ocean waves crashing on to a beach. Finally, when Minister Farrakhan stepped to the podium, the crowd erupted with such thunderous applause and loud cheering, that it seemed as if the earth trembled under the weight of our love and adulation for the man. I have heard, since the march, many a claim by white and black news reporters that they were told, when interviewing various march attendees, that many of the men had confided that they had not come to the capital specifically to hear Minister Lewis Farrakhan, but for more personal reasons. All I can say to that is, they certainly didn't interview any of the hundreds of men with whom I spoke. Furthermore, judging the reaction of the crowd to Minister Farrakhan, I sincerely doubt whether those reporters were even at the same march that I attended.

Minister Farrakhan was the personification of love, compassion and forgiveness. He seemed to be the embodiment of that which represents the absolute best in all of us. He talked of the black man's degradation and dehumanization at the hands of white America. Then he talked of the utter insanity of white supremacy, the philosophy that has dominated America's attitude and shaped her public policy toward the black man since his arrival on these shores. He explained why white supremacy must be destroyed if America and the rest of the world are to survive. Then he talked about the black man's responsibility for his own salvation, and the survival of his family. He told us that we must develop our own community, create our own jobs, eliminate the crime in our own neighborhoods, and that we must provide for and protect our women and children. He challenged us to be honest enough to admit that we have failed in our responsibilities to our families and stand up at last and be the kind of real men that our women and children can truly respect and be proud of. Farrakhan's words seemed to have struck a resounding chord of conviction, confirmation and confidence in the souls of all of us as we witnessed the truth of his words and confirmed his testimony with honest heart felt ovations.

Furthermore, he challenged us to go back to our communities and get busy. He articulated some of the programs that the Nation of Islam was engaged in to bring about the kind of change that he had talked

250

about for more than two hours. He encouraged us to go back and get involved with our churches, Mosques, Synagogues, lodges, and any other organization that works for the genuine benefit of black people. Then he reached out in conciliation to all those black leaders who had denounced him and urged black men to stay away from the march. He also extended an invitation to Jewish leaders to sit down with him and try to reconcile those differences that have, for so long polarized the two groups. Finally, he implored white Americans to abandon the sick philosophy of white supremacy and race hatred that has created and maintained the gulf between the two groups in America. Minister Farrakhan was superb in every sense of the word. He spoke from the moral high ground that is simply unheard of from leaders these days. He has emerged as the kind of genuine statesman that is worthy of being called a leader. He has been on the front line, struggling for black people for the last four decades. As a result, he has earned the love and respect of his people by daring to tell the unpleasant truth about their pitiful condition, even at the risk of his own personal safety and public reputation. He has stood tall, firm, strong and he has passionately articulated the frustrations and aspirations of his people. Still, he has not wavered, even when other, so called black leaders have been tripping over each other to distance themselves from him. This is why I was one in a million in Washington D.C. on October 16, 1995. This is why I deeply admire and greatly respect Minister Lewis Farrakhan. In my opinion, he is the only true leader black or white living today in America who is even worthy of the title.

Although the march was co-sponsored by Minister Lewis Farrakhan and the Reverend Ben Chavis, the white press tried its best to isolate Minister Farrakhan and portray the whole idea as a project of the Nation of Islam. Unfortunately, the media was quite successful in it's smear campaign of depicting Minister Farrakhan as a hate monger. White reporters on every major television news program tried their best to bate, beguile, and trap him into confirming their slanderous reports on the Nation of Islam and their contemptuous opinions of him. Time and again, the minister handled himself with such intellectual brilliance, he exposed them for the race-baiting demagogues that they are. With his unassailable knowledge of facts, irrefutable logic, and splendid oratory, they were overwhelmed. With cool headed self-possession and the unshakable self-confidence rarely seen in any black man in America, Farrakhan's dedication and commitment to the righteousness of his cause, equipped him to passionately and eloquently articulate the pain and suffering of the great masses of black people in this nation. He was able to do this in their media, despite the best efforts of a host of rabidly racist and openly hostile reporters, who were ready to vilify and discredit him at every turn. This is why the great majority of black men and women listened to and responded to his call, despite the best efforts on the part of the press and other black leaders to keep them away. Yet, the media was, as I have stated, quite successful in reaching those handkerchief head house slaves who, like their predecessors on the plantation, worked overtime to discourage other blacks from participating in the march. Fortunately, they

252

failed, and failed miserably. They learned perhaps for the first time, that the common masses of black men and women were through with their weak-kneed, cowardly, shuffling, Uncle Tom, hat-in-hand leadership. Tragically, the national Baptist Convention was staunchly against the march. It is the largest black religious organization in the nation. Then why was its leadership so adamantly against the Million-man March? According to its president, Rev. Henry Lyons, in a statement he made to an affiliate of National Public Radio on the eve of the march, "Our differences theologically, are too deep. Based on our beliefs, there is no point in which we can walk with the Nation of Islam and brother Farrakhan." Later in a speech he gave at the Mount Zion Missionary Baptist Church, one of the largest and oldest black churches in Miami, Minister Farrakhan chastised the black clergy who refused to support the march.

Yet, these black clergy had accepted an apology from a white southern Baptist organization for once supporting slavery. "I would like to ask the Baptists," Farrakhan said, "Who were the white Baptists that lynched us? They've run you out of the Baptist Church. So, today they give you some little weak apology, and you can walk behind them, but you can't walk with your brother, who never did anything but good for you." The minister went on to point out how intellectually irrational and morally dishonest those black preachers were by their spiritually unethical stance of non-support for the Million-Man March. He also pointed out that they were continuing to walk in lock step with those who have historically, and continue to oppress black people. Those super sanctimo-

253

nious Negroes had no problem finding the grace in their holy, hollow hearts to forgive those white folk who had not only supported human slavery, but were now the direct beneficiaries of that damnable system of human misery. However, they just couldn't bring themselves to accept and support Lewis Farrakhan. How ironic? How ethically incongruent? How intellectually dishonest? How logically indefensible? How spiritually reprehensible? So, Lyons advised the thirty three thousand pastors in his organization not to take part in the Million-Man March.

This, by and large, was the reaction of the entire black church establishment. The only other black clergy of note who actually supported the march were the Rev. Jesse Jackson and the Rev. Joseph Lowrey. However, prior to the eve of the march, even their support was little more than lukewarm Jackson had originally claimed that he wouldn't be able to participate in the march due to a scheduling conflict. Likewise, Lowrey had offered some convenient excuse for not participating. Nevertheless, both men managed to find the time to participate and even became miraculously enthusiastic when it became apparent to them that the march was going to be a phenomenal success. Predictably, the Urban League and NAACP, as well as every other so called, (main stream black organization) was vehemently opposed to the Million-Man March, allegedly because of Minister Lewis Farrakhan's participation. I quote the late Malcolm X, "We don't catch hell in America because we are Baptists, Methodists, Catholics, or belong to the Nation of Islam. We catch hell in America, because we're black." I would also add to that statement, the same goes for those of us who belong to the NAACP, the Urban League, and any other black fraternal, professional, social, or political organization in America. This great gathering of black men, in an effort to come together and solve those problems which threaten our survival, finally exposed all of those "Closet Uncle Toms", for the heartless, spineless, shuffling, grinning and bowing, "House Negroes", that they really are.

This cowardly wholesale abandonment of the genuine interest of the great masses of African-Americans on the part of the black church was never more glaringly evident and poignantly striking, than against the back drop of the Million-Man March. What rational thinking, intellectually honest, and morally sound African-American could seriously and legitimately justify not participating in, or at least embracing the idea of the Million -Man March? Those ever grinning, handkerchief head, shuffling boot-licking, house Negro demagogues who are convinced that they've got it made, who were so vehemently opposed to the Million Man March, merely exposed themselves to the rest of us, for what they truly are. They tried to justify their scurrilous behavior by hiding behind the baseless notion furnished to them by the white press, that the march was Farrakhan's idea and a project controlled exclusively by the Nation of Islam. So they worked overtime trying to derail the effort to promote and organize the march. Fortunately, they failed. Let's say, for the sake of argument, that the march was indeed totally Minister Farrakhan's idea. Did that make those spiritual imperatives that he called for any less valid or legitimate?

255

Simply because Lewis Farrakhan called for the spiritual atonement of black men, did that make the need for such atonement any less acute? Just because Minister Farrakhan beckoned black men to the nation's capital in an effort to get them to see the need to clean up their communities, support their wives and children, and stop the pandemic violence against each other, did that make the over arching need for black men to honestly address these things any less critical and necessary? I emphatically submit that it certainly did not! So, all the lame, baseless, and totally self-serving excuses not to support the march, that those "House Negroes" could manufacture along with those provided them by their plantation bosses simply do not hold water.

This is why the present black clergy should not and must not continue to dominate the church. It is simply too spiritually dysfunctional and morally bankrupt to do any thing constructive, positive, or morally redeeming in the African-American community. It has demonstrated over and over again, that it lacks the spiritual heart, moral courage, or intellectual honesty to lead anyone, anywhere. It is too thoroughly lost, too spiritually dead, too pathetically hypocritical, and too bereft of any genuine moral conscience to lead the church. These so called preacher: are simply not called by God, or sent by him to do anything, because if they were, they would be imbued with the Spirit of God and doing the will of God. Their actions would consequently demonstrate the true love of god. Just who are these Godless infidels to say that Lewis Farrakhan is not morally qualified to speak on behalf of the millions of suffering black fol who have no voice in America? God can use whomever he will or may, to articulate the voiceless anguish of the suffering masses and bring his divine truth to this pathetically corrupt and hopelessly wicked generation. So if those who claim to love him and have professed to the world, to have his Holy Spirit, are in fact, nothing but lying hypocrites, then God will and often does, use whomever he chooses to get his message to his people. I was at that march, and I felt the presence of the Holy Spirit of god there. That march and the message of that march were larger than Lewis Farrakhan, or any one man.

Anyone who had even an inkling of conscience or god in his or her soul could have easily seen that. Then the man's message of love, forgiveness, and reconciliation came straight out of the Christian tradition which is predicated on the so called, "Born Again", experience. This is the creed of Christianity, the religion that the great majority of Americans, white and black, claim so piously to embrace. Yet, the black clergy and the great majority of non-African-Americans alike viewed, Lewis Farrakhan, as a religious pariah. His message was viewed with nothing but scorn and contempt. However, this vicious and vitriolic response only illuminated and highlighted the abject poverty of spirit and wickedness of soul of these infidels who are bound and determined to keep the great masses of African-Americans locked in a racial caste as a permanent and powerless under class in this nation. We must ask ourselves, who stands to benefit by maintaining this sorry state of affairs in the black community? Well let me tell you, those non black owned banks and other lending institutions who take

257

black folks' money and invest that money outside of the black community and make enormous corporate profits for their owners and share holders. Then they will simultaneously refuse mortgage and business loans to those same residents whose money they use to create their enormous profits. Then there are those absentee Slum Lords who get rich charging exorbitant rents for substandard dwellings that should be condemned. There is also the multi-billion dollar drug trade that has fueled the trade and concomitant profit in automatic assault weapons, which have flooded the black community. These military weapons should not be in the hands of civilians, especially, angry, ignorant, misguided, and impressionable young black men who seem to think it is a right of passage and badge of machismo to murder other blacks.

Hollywood has made huge profits off of movies depicting young blacks as amoral, ruthless, and sadistic killers, especially of other blacks. The powerful images portraying these so called black gangsters as hard, tough, and glamorous role models, have thoroughly warped the minds and profoundly distorted the perceptions of a whole generation of black youth. They seem to be totally unaware that they have been duped into thinking that it is cool, hip, and even macho to engage in such morally reprehensible and physically destructive behavior. The record industry has behaved just as reprehensibly toward the black community. From the sexually explicit and ruthlessly vulgar lyrics, to the scantily clad women in the videos black artists try to out do each other to see who can be the sleaziest, raunchiest, and most degrading in their music. However, whenever they are challenged o

258

taken to task for their antisocial and morally bankrupt behavior, they rush to hide behind the specious arguments of realism and artistic freedom.

In point of fact, these recording artists, if they can be called artists, are nothing but empty hearted, greedy men and women who are willing to degrade, dehumanize, and humiliate themselves and all other black people in order to make a dollar. So they endeavor to concoct all manner of pseudo-intellectual arguments in a vain attempt to mask their naked greed and relentless lust for material success. Consequently, they have abandoned all pretense of principle, ethics, and morality in their frantic pursuit of the almighty Dollar. As a result, they have allowed themselves to be prostituted and exploited in the worst possible way by those who have no real use for them except as puppets, buffoons, and self-deprecating clowns in black face to be used as economic commodities. There is absolutely no excuse for us not to challenge those pathetic African-Americans who are so bereft of any sense of identity, self-worth, and ethnic consciousness that they will do anything under the guise of art and entertainment as long as they can get paid. How spiritually, morally, and psychologically pathetic! What's even more tragic about this whole sick syndrome, is that all of the record artists and nearly all of the film- makers who have been so pathetically scandalous in the degradation of black men and women, are African-American, themselves.

However, when they are taken to task for the creation and promotion of such grotesque violence and indefensible filth, they invariably try to hide behind the sham defense of realism and freedom of artistic expression. Consequently, it is not difficult to understand why white folk do not respect us. Why should they? Why should any one respect African-Americans when it is painfully obvious that we have virtually no respect for ourselves. There is absolutely no reason that sober minded, rationally thinking, morally sound, and above all self-respecting black men and women should allow those unethical reprobates among us to degrade and dehumanize us before the world. This ruthless castigation of black men by these so called artist, as fools, dogs, niggers, and every other epithet that their warped minds can conceive, is simply despicable. It is even more despicable that African-American men and women in good conscience can sit back and allow it.

Furthermore, the absolute trampling of black womanhood by referring to African-American women as whores, bitches, and anything else that these so call artists can think of just as disrespectful and derogatory, must be stopped at all cost. It is past time that we, who know that there is no earthly justification for this kind of self-flagellating, self-deprecating, and thoroughly self-destructive behavior stand up and put an end to this insanity. We must rise up in vehement opposition and sanction those pathetically misguided black men and women among us for their vicious assault on the dignity of our people hood. Why? Because it is the right, moral, and just thing to do. If we would only stop and consider how ludicrous we must look to non African-Americans in our vaunted demand for respect, when we allow those morally bankrupt individuals, right in our own
260

group, to consistently humiliate, degrade, and dehumanize us before the whole world. Most African-Americans are instantly moved to anger and indignation when a white person refers to them or another black person as a nigger. How ironic! Many of us use that despicable word all the time. Paradoxically, it seems to be some how palatable to us whenever it issues from the lips of another black person.

There is a steady stream of movies written, produced by, and starring blacks that are replete with the most vulgar themes and profane language. Moreover, these movies feature, promote, and reinforce the most torrid and vicious racial stereotypes and myths about blacks. For instance, blacks are either, portrayed as clowns, minstrels, pimps, drug dealers, vicious murderers, or insatiable studs engaging in promiscuous sex. These worthless pieces of trash palmed off on the African-American community as art, have severely distorted the perception and shaped the behavior in the most negative ways possible, of a whole generation of young black people. The dominant message in the great majority of black music and movies seemed to encourage the relentless pursuit of drugs, alcohol, sexual pleasure, gold chains, designer clothes, fancy cars, and automatic weapons: the quintessential goals for success. These horrific weapons, which have been dumped into the inner cities across this nation, have literally created war zones as gangs fight it out for turf, which neither can legitimately claim. Nevertheless, they fight each other and terrorize helpless, hopeless, and desperate people who are caught in the crossfire. These assault weapons along with crack cocaine, placed in the hands of such young, ignorant, and hopelessly misguided black youth have been the prescription for disaster in our community. These military weapons should not be in a civilian population, under any circumstance, except to promote murder and mayhem. Therefore, with the proliferation of street gangs, these weapons have done nothing but promote a form of tribalism in the black community. They have given young black men and women the ability to murder each other more efficiently. Finally, there is the national boom in prison construction fueled by the violence, murder, and general carnage in the black community. A recent study revealed that nearly one in three African-American males between the ages of twenty and twenty-nine, are under some form of criminal justice supervision. They are either, in prison, in jail, on probation, or on parole. The report also revealed, to no one surprise, that in the African-American community, African-Americans are being punished disproportionately in the so-called, war on drugs. Black Americans make up only thirteen percent of drug users, but they represent fifty five percent of drug convictions and seventy four percent of prison sentences. The report went on to say that inner cities are targeted for drug arrests. Almost nine out of ten defendants prosecuted under the new federal (Crack Cocaine) law are black. Furthermore, (Crack Cocaine) carries a far harsher sentence than powdered cocaine. Needless to say, crack cocaine is far more prevalent in the black community.

One answer, suggested in the report, was that less money should be spent on law enforcement and more on prevention and treatment in inner cities.

This was an approach endorsed by former Drug Czar, Lee Brown. However, Congress has consistently proposed less money for drug prevention and more money for block grants and prisons. Even the majority of the bars, carry out shops, and liquor stores, the most stable and profitable businesses in the black community, are not owned, for the most part, by the residents of the community. So, now I ask the question once again, who really is benefiting from the social, and economic disorganization of the African-American community? So, let those mortal enemies of black people, go on and criticize Lewis Farrakhan and all those others who are sincerely trying to improve the sorry condition of the great masses of black folk in this racist nation. We know who you are and we know why you behave as you do. We understand all to well that you white supremacists who run America will use any means at your disposal to prevent any constructive political, social, spiritual, or economic improvement in the lives of the masses of black people in this nation. We know that you will even use other Negroes in order to help you keep the masses of black folk in their place. Who are these white supremacists? They are those who own more than fifty five percent of the nation's wealth and who dominate and hold the reins of governmental and corporate power in America. Those who believe in and are fanatically committed to the proposition that white folk are innately superior to black people and want to see this philosophy thoroughly implemented and rigidly maintained in every aspect of American life. Therefore, they have created and maintained a superior status for whites and an inferior status, or racial caste, for blacks.

This economic stratification based on skin color has been rigidly enforced in every area of American life since the African's arrival on these shores. This is why so many white people, who are not rich and powerful, are so vehemently opposed to any effort on the part of the government to assist blacks through affirmative action programs. They seem to have no trouble at all over looking the fact that it was the myriad racially oppressive and economically discriminatory policies of the federal and state governments that created and maintained the racial caste system for blacks in this nation for centuries. This is the primary reason for our current miserable economic plight in America. These white people vehemently oppose any efforts on the part of this government in its attempts to redress the historical denial of black opportunity by creating Affirmative Action programs to enable African-Americans to gain equal access to economic opportunity. They fear the prospect that black people may be economically elevated to a status equal to their own. Never mind that the great majority of white people in America have been robbed of economic opportunity and treated almost as badly by the white elite as blacks have been treated. They continue to staunchly support that same elite that they can only identify with vicariously by virtue of their white skin. So the poor white man has been duped into believing that the black man is his nemesis, just waiting to take his job, his woman, and move into his neighborhood.

As a result, the poor white man becomes consumed with hatred for the black man and vents his feelings through his vote by supporting every righ wing conservative politician that he can find. These demagogues, whom he believes, are his friends will make laws and institute economic policies that will also, just as thoroughly as they do to poor blacks, rob him of economic opportunity. However, he has been thoroughly duped by the white elite, into adopting its racist attitudes and politics that have in fact systematically worked to his detriment. So by constantly raising the issue of skin color, and perpetuating the racist dogma of black inferiority, the white elite of America has for generations, convinced poor white people to adopt their attitudes and politics, but they have never shared their great wealth with them. So let the spiritually dead talk, let those who walk in eternal darkness talk, because the scriptures ask, what does darkness have in common with light. II Cor. 6:14-18. Consequently, what would the sons of Satan know about the grace of God? There was such a profound spirit of love, hope, compassion, and respect that enveloped that gathering, and for once, simply over shadowed all of the petty differences that we black folk use to divide ourselves.

At least on the day of that march we were all on one accord. No one, but the Divine Spirit of God, could have accomplished that kind of unanimity among a people so totally lost, thoroughly confused, and so ruthlessly manipulated by others. There was genuine unity among us on that day in Washington D.C. This was really what frightened so many white people, but not Minister Lewis Farrakhan. He was merely used as a lightening rod for white America's vitriolic hysteria in its attempt to prevent the manifestation, and possible consolidation, of that kind of gen-

265

uine unity among black people. White people realize and can appreciate the awesome power of unity and organization. Why it has been their unique ability to organize and come together as a group that has enabled them to dominate and control this whole planet. However, they are determined to prevent this kind of organization and unity from happening among African-Americans. Therefore when any African-American like Marcus Garvey, Elijah Muhammad, Martin Luther King, Malcolm X, and of late Lewis Farrakhan emerges and shows the potential of actually organizing a significant number of black people, white America work over time to destroy him. Such leaders have historically been dealt with in one of four ways: discredited and bought down by character assassination, co-opted into the system and effectively neutralized, made the victim of out right assassination, or imprisonment. The fact of the matter is, that those white supremacists, who have run America since its inception have historically been, and continue to be, totally dedicated to the destruction of any semblance of genuine trust, respect, or cooperation among black people. If we were allowed to actually create any semblance of genuine trust in each other, respect for one another, or conscious cooperation with each other, we could indeed organize and achieve that elusive dream of self-determination. Then we could, like other ethnic groups in this nation, control the economics and politics of our own community. We would therefore not be dependent on, or thoroughly controlled by non African-Americans for our survival.

The fact that those black ministers who urged their congregations to stay away from the march could not see through this dastardly effort by the white press to prevent this unity, only testifies as to how hopelessly lost they really are. This also clearly confirms how easily manipulated they can be by those racist demagogues whose only real use for them is that of tool and fool. God is a god of wisdom, not foolishness, compassion, not contempt, and mercy for his suffering people, not the monstrous manipulation of them. The fact of the matter is, that the great majority of African-Americans are suffering miserably in this nation. For those who claim to be leaders of millions of those suffering souls, to tell black Americans to stay away from a convocation convened by someone who is sincerely trying to find solutions for their suffering, is nothing short of criminal. As I have stated before, this event called, the Million-Man march, poignantly underscored the fact that the black clergy, by and large, is nothing but a chorus line of tools and fools, dancing to the tune of the white power structure in this nation. They are nothing more than puppets mouthing the words and dancing to the music of their puppeteers, who are their white masters. They are a scurvy class of hopeless hypocrites and merciless parasites perpetrating the vilest sins against the very people that they so pompously and piously profess to serve.

Yes, they are those who have prostituted the word of God and perpetrated the worst crime of all. These are those wolves in sheep clothing, those wicked infidels who shall have their reward in the lake of fire with the only true god of their reprobated souls, Satan. They are the absolute worst enemies of Jesus Christ, African-Americans, and oppressed people everywhere. They are nothing but a clergy for hire.

267

They are a morally reprehensible lot of hopeless hypocrites who are indeed in the service of Satan. He is their true father.

CHAPTER 16

From Theory to Practice

I submit that the greatest weakness of the African-American church today is its pathetic inability or unwillingness to translate the theory of Christianity into its practical application. I believe that the fundamental reasons for such an assertion have already been articulated and overwhelmingly substantiated. My reasons have been enumerated during my discussion on previous pages about the character and orientation of the great majority of the black church's leadership. Consequently, the logical conclusion which flows from such an equation, given the low caliber and misguided orientation of the overwhelming majority of the black clergy, coupled with the most extreme elements, such as the pimp, punk, and pusher, the leadership falls far short of the qualifications necessary for the task.

First of all, as I have said before, there has never been a spiritually sincere, nor intellectually honest, nor rationally sound analysis of the Bible by African-American church leaders. They have simply regurgitated the same old distorted, disjointed, convoluted, and thoroughly racists interpretation of the Bible that has been handed down to them by their slave masters. As a result, they continue to cling tenaciously to the interpretation of the bible that has been used to bestialize black folk and justify their enslavement.

Moreover, their Theological Seminary education has only served to make them more effective promoters of the same racist dogma that still seeks to justify the dehumanization and exploitation of African-Americans. Even after the abolition of legal slavery, the racist mentality that forms the bases of religious doctrine in this nation, remained a fluid part of American culture, which reinforced the black man's social status as an ethnic inferior. Through the eyes of this western European version of Christianity, the black man and his kind are seen as the cursed children of Ham and their lot on this earth is to be the drawers of water and hewers of wood and servants to the lighter skinned European ethnics. In other words, they are to occupy that inferior status in America's racial caste that white supremacists have designated as, "the nigger's place." Genesis 9:18-27: This kind of pseudo-religious nonsense has been used to justify the most sadistic degradation, dehumanization, and exploitation of black peoples all over the world for centuries. Yet, the victims of it, the black clergy, still insist upon clinging to this absurdly ludicrous myth as if it were indeed historically valid, intellectually legitimate, or a spiritually eternal truth.

This is why they are totally unfit to be the spiritual leaders of black people. They are lost and in great need of divine deliverance from their own psychologically crippling and spiritually withering slave mentality. They have indoctrinated with, and internalized a body of grotesquely distorted religious dogma, which only makes them servile lackeys of a white power elite, which never has, and never will accept the cursed children of Ham, as social equals. Therefore, the African-

270

American clergy is an extension of the same religious dogma that continues to keep African-Americans spiritually dysfunctional, emotionally disconnected from their African heritage, and psychologically alienated from their true African selves.

The majority of these black church leaders are very pious in their ignorance, and hostile to the notion that they may not have a monopoly on the whole truth. So with their white washed minds and sanctimonious pomposity, they go forth spouting the same old brain dead, convoluted, ridiculous and thoroughly racist religious dogma which has been passed down to them by their slave masters. Therefore, those sincere souls who are fed up with this empty rhetoric and spiritually gilded gospel spewed forth by these servile underlings of the white political power elite, must find the way for themselves. Those who have the spirit and wisdom of Jesus Christ living in their souls, know that these cowardly, handkerchief-head, grinning and shuffling, political puppets are more lost, themselves, than the people that they are trying to lead.

First of all, in order to translate the theory of Christianity into its appropriate and proper practical application, one must be dedicated to a systematic study and rational analysis of the scriptures. Above all things we must get an understanding. Proverbs 4:7: "Wisdom is the principal thing, therefore get wisdom: and with all thy getting, get understanding." Therefore, we must never rely solely on one source for such important Biblical information, especially an interpretation offered by those who have used that information as a tool to enslave and exploit people.

271

We must consult other versions of the bible, even those written in other languages. We must also endeavor to investigate and understand what events were taking place in the world during the time that the various books of the Bible were written. Moreover, we must analyze those events of antiquity that may have had some impact on the way that the Bible was compiled. Also, we must recognize and appreciate the fact that the Bible has been distorted and perverted through its many translations over the centuries. This is the primary reason that the black man, who was the original subject, has been all but written out of the Bible. It is imperative that we get an understanding of the true physical facts about the historical Jesus before we can ever hope to comprehend the true significance of the spiritual Jesus. Also we must get a clear understanding of the role of the African in the Bible. The Black man has been all but totally omitted from the Western European version. So, there is a tremendous amount of study and research involved in ascertaining the true and full meaning of the Bible.

Next we have to understand the difference between religiosity and spirituality. These two things are not necessarily the same. However I believe that they have been thoroughly confused by clergy who hardly understand the meaning of either. Religiosity involves the rituals that are used in the public practice of a given religion. For example, it is the style, method, and form of worship, as well as other nuances of the actual practice of any given religion, which can be outwardly observed. The regular or systematic observance or practice of these rituals is an expression of one religiosity. However, spirituality involves whether

272

or not an individual has established an intimate relationship with God and has actually submitted himself or herself to his divine will and purpose on this earth. Whether or not an individual truly establishes an intimate relationship with God and then allows himself to be led by his Holy Spirit, is not necessarily predicated on the mere practice and observance of religious ritual. The scripture declares in John 4:24: that, God is a spirit; and they that worship Him must worship in spirit and truth. Jesus said, in John 15:5-7: "I am the vine, ye are the branches. He that abideth in me, and I in him, the same bringeth forth much fruit; for without me ye can do nothing. If ye abide in me, and my word abide in you, ye shall ask what you will, and it shall be done unto you." Jesus also declared, that his Disciples would be known by their fruit. John 6:16-20: He made it very clear as to how a true Christian is supposed to behave by actually spelling out the specific qualities that should be present in a Christian's life. Then he delineated the fruit of the flesh and contrasted that with the fruit of the spirit. Galatians 5:19-23: "Now the works of the flesh are manifest, which are these: adultery, fornication, uncleanness, lasciviousness, Idolatry, witchcraft, hatred, avarice, emulation, wrath, strife, sedition, heresies, envy, murder, drunkenness, reveling, and such like: with that which I tell you before, as I have also told you in times past, they which do such things shall not inherit the kingdom of God. But the fruit of the spirit is love, joy, peace, suffering, gentleness, goodness, and faith; meekness and, temperance: against such there is no law." Gal. 5: 24-26: "If we live in the spirit, let us also walk in the spirit." Therefore if an individual has truly established and maintains an intimate relationship with Christ, as a result of that relationship, then corresponding fruit of the spirit should then be manifest in his or her life. Furthermore, when one is honest and sincere enough to, accept Jesus Christ as his or her Lord and Savior, and is obedient enough to submit to His divine will, then there will be a corresponding transformation of character and focus. II Cor. 5: 14-17: Verse 17: "Therefore if any man be in Christ, he is a new creature: old things are passed away; behold, all things are become new." However, this transformation is in direct proportion to the extent that the individual has accepted and submitted to the divine will of Christ.

Well, how does one really establish an intimate relationship with Christ? Romans Chapter 10, verse 9 ," If thou shalt confess with thy mouth to the Lord Jesus, and shalt believe in thy heart that God hath raised him from the dead, thou shall be saved." Verse 10 "For with the heart, man believeth unto righteousness: and with the mouth confession is made unto salvation." This is the act of true belief in Jesus Christ as Lord and Savior. Then there must be a genuine repentance for sin and the subsequent invitation to Christ to come into one heart and be the Lord of one life. Now the act of repentance must mean more than just merely saying that one is sorry for his or her sins. Moreover, he or she must make a sincere promise to Christ not to continue in sin. Now, if this individual is sincere in his or her actions, the spirit of Jesus Christ will come into his or her heart and give him or her the power to change through the indwelling of His Holy Spirit. There is absolutely, positively no way an individual can have victory over sin and Satan in this life without the power of Christ's indwelling Holy Spirit. However, once a relationship with God is established, it must be strengthened and cultivated through total submission to his will, consistent prayer, meditation, and study of the scriptures. God promised that if an individual would draw nigh to Him, He would reciprocate. James 4:6-8. This is how we learn in a real sense, exactly who God is. The requirements for accomplishing an intimate relationship with God are no different from the principles involved in establishing an intimate human friendship. Our best friends are those with whom we spend treasured quantity and quality time. As a result, of this shared experience, we grow to respect, love, trust, and feel that we can depend on these friends, even if all others forsake us.

This kind of intimate relationship, however, is always borne out of treasured quantity and quality time. It is strengthened over time into a deep love and trust through years of shared experiences. How can we really expect to have an intimate relationship with Jesus Christ without taking the time that is required in daily prayer, study, periodic fasting, and meditation. However, He also said that he who promises to do His will and doeth it not is a liar and the truth is not in him. I John 2:4-5: " He that saith, I know him and keepeth not his commandments, is a liar, and the truth is not in him. But who so keepeth his word, in him verily is the love of God perfected: hereby know we that we are in him." He also said, "He who knoweth to do right and doeth it not, shall be beaten with many stripes". Luke 12:47-48: Therefore, the presence or absence of a relationship with Jesus Christ will invariably reflect in ones attitude and behavior toward his or her fellow man. Jesus Christ said that the world will know the Christians by the love that they will show one for another. John 13: 34-35: "A new commandment I give unto you, That ye love one another: as I have loved you, that ye also love one another. By this shall all men know that ye are my disciples, if ye have love one to another." Therefore, Jesus Christ's fundamental requirements for true Christian discipleship are found right here in these verses. These are the unalterable criteria for genuine Christian discipleship that can only be achieved if one has honestly accepted Christ as Lord and savior.

Many have tried to perfect this persona of Christian discipleship by imitation, and pretense. However, under the divine scrutiny of the Holy Spirit, their best efforts are tantamount to nothing more than a pitiful sham. Consequently, at the core of a true Christian life is first, a genuine love for God, and then a genuine love for one fellow man. There is also total obedience to the will of God. The kind of carnal minded and conditional love that comes naturally to us is not at all what Jesus means when he talks about love. On the contrary, he is talking about that agape love, a kind of self-sacrificing love, that divine and eternal love that can only be obtained as a result of an intimate relationship with God. This kind of love can only emanate from the spirit of God living in the heart and soul of one who has honestly accepted Jesus Christ as Lord and Savior. Ephesians 1:13 "In whom ye also trusted, after that ye heard that word of truth, the gospel of your salvation; in whom ye also after that ye believed, ye were sealed with the holy

276

Spirit of promise." So, being a Christian is not something that you do on Sunday, or whenever you are in church. On the contrary, it is something that you are. It is your character, the disposition of your soul, the essence of what and who you are and the total way that you live. It is the result of your intimate relationship with Jesus Christ. Furthermore, it involves whether or not you have made a conscious and willful decision to make Jesus Christ Lord of your life and are allowing his Holy Spirit to live and reign supreme in your soul.

The difficulty in labeling someone a Christian, is the inability to distinguish style from substance. Far too many folk believe that church attendance, church work, or church affiliation, is synonymous with Christian discipleship. In fact, nothing can be further from the truth. As I have stated before, religiosity does not a Christian make. Most so called, "Christians", only have what I call, a Psychosocial attitude toward Christianity. This means that they are obsessed with effecting the appearance of a Christian lifestyle through regular church attendance. This makes them feel as if they are actually living Christian lives. They immerse themselves in, "church work", such as singing in the choir, serving on the usher board, teaching Sunday school, leading prayer service, serving in the nurses corps, and in any number of other church auxiliaries. These activities are performed so as to convince themselves and others, that they are, in fact and in deed, doing God's work. They feel that this qualifies them as Christians. They feel that their dedication and faithfulness to duty in these things is the same as living a sanctified life and being Holy before God. On the contrary, this is nothing more than an effective orientation to Christianity. Why? Because these individuals feel that they are Christians by virtue of their church work. However, this has absolutely nothing to do with whether they have actually accepted Jesus Christ as Savior and honestly made Him Lord of their lives. Anything short of this sincere acceptance of, and total submission to Jesus Christ, is only pretense, self-delusion, and religiosity.

It is the confusion of work and duty with spirituality and Holiness. It is works without faith, which is just as bad as faith without works. James 2:26 "For as the body without the spirit is dead, so faith without works is dead also." No amount of work or dedication to ritual or duty can substitute for a truly born again soul living a Holy and Sanctified life. In other words, no amount of pious pretension, pompous posturing, or pseudo-sanctimony, can substitute for an honest acceptance of Christ and submission to his divine will. This is the only way to sanctification, justification, and Holy living. This and only this can produce the true fruit of the spirit, which can only be made manifest in one life as a result of that intimate relationship with Jesus Christ. Jesus Christ's requirement for discipleship is Holiness and sanctification. This is the only way an individual can possibly fulfill Christ's requirement for Christian discipleship and live up right and righteously before God and man. Hebrews 12:14. This has nothing to do with whether or not an individual sings in the choir, teaches Sunday school serves on the usher board, nurse's corps or leads the prayer service. God is concerned with whether or no
278

there has been a genuine conversion of the heart and whether the individual is walking in the newness of life, which should be the evidence of that conversion.

Is the individual really living a born again, Holy and sanctified life? Is the individual really producing the fruit of the Spirit in his or her life, or is he or she still producing the fruit of the flesh? Unless there has been a genuine acceptance of Jesus Christ as one Lord and savior, and a sincere desire to submit to His divine will, there can be no fundamental change or genuine spiritual growth. This is why millions of people who have been devoutly involved in their churches for years, have not had any qualitative spiritual growth in their lives. As a result, they talk one thing and live quite something else. These are they whom the Lord will rebuke in the judgment saying depart from me ye workers of iniquity. Matt. 7:21-23: "And then will I profess unto them, I never knew you. Depart from me, ye that work iniquity." This psychological exercise in self-deception remains nothing more than an emotional flight into fantasy, form, and fashion and is totally devoid of spiritual substance. This kind of emotional game playing without any real sincere dedication to or acceptance of Jesus Christ as Lord and Savior makes for the kind of Sunday morning saints, hopeless hypocrisy, and lukewarm Christendom that is the bedrock of western Christianity.

It is impossible to fake spirituality. One either has accepted Christ as Lord and Savior, received the Holy spirit and has a relationship with God, or one has not. This fact will invariably show in one attitude and personality. Jesus said in Matt. 3-13, "There will be many who will come in the last days and say, Lord, did I not cast out demons in your name and I will say depart from me ye workers of inequity." Paul said, "Let the mind of Christ be that mind in you." Philippians 2: 1-8: "If there be therefore any consolation in Christ, any comfort of love, any fellowship of the Spirit, any bowels and mercies." "Fulfill ye my joy, that ye be like-minded, having the same love, being of one accord, of one mind." "Let this mind be in you, which was also in Christ Jesus." Paul also stressed, in Romans 12:1, "I Beseech you therefore, brethren, by the mercies of God, ye present your body a living sacrifice, holy acceptable unto God, which is your reasonable service." Furthermore, Christ said, "I would that ye were hot or cold, but because ye are lukewarm, I will spew you out of my mouth." Rev. 3:14-22: "I know thy works, that thou art neither cold nor hot. I would thou were cold or hot. So then because thou art lukewarm, and neither cold nor hot, I will spew thee out of my mouth." The scriptures clearly point out the requirements of discipleship. However, most people who call themselves Christians are too dishonest to confront these requirements. They simply have no intentions of accepting Jesus Christ as their Lord and Savior or submitting to His divine will. Therefore, they engage in intellectual dishonesty, and psychological self-delusion. Their interpretation of the Bible allows them to delude themselves into thinking that they are something that they are not. Christ said that if we truly love Him, then we would keep His commandments. As a result, when we piously declare to the world how much we love Him, and not keep his commandments, He declares that we are liars. I John 2:4 says, "He that saith, I know him and keepeth not his commandments, is a liar, and the truth is not in him."

So, I submit that the most fundamental prerequisites for obtaining genuine spirituality are intellectual honesty, and then spiritual sincerity. We all know in our secret hearts when we are wrong, when we do wrong, and whether or not we actually know Jesus Christ. We also know if we honestly have any desire to really submit to His divine will for our lives. Further more, I submit that Jesus Christ Himself has made this abundantly clear in the parable about the rich young ruler and the treasure a man found in a field. These can be found in Matthew 19:16-26. and Matthew 13:44. He often chided the Pharisees by pointing out the glaring discrepancy between their devotion to religious ritual and their absence of genuine spirituality. In other words, He explained to them over and over that they were indeed devoutly religious in their observance of the law but they were sorely lacking in spirituality. In other words, they had no relationship with God. Therefore, it was impossible for them to have the true love of God, understand the mind of God, or be guided by the Spirit of God. So for all their meticulous attention and fanatical devotion to the observance of the law, Jesus called them whited tombs full of dead men's bones. He excoriated them for all their religious piety and how they failed to connect with the spirit of God which could have led them into truth and put them in a right relationship with God and their fellowmen. Instead, they chose to believe themselves righteous because of their observance of the law. Christ tried to tell them the law kills, but the spirit quickens or brings life.

Therefore it is only through an individual's sincere belief that God exists and an honest effort to seek and worship Him in spirit and in truth by being born again of water and of the spirit, can a true relationship with God be established. John 3:1-7: Jesus answered, "Verily, Verily, I say unto thee, except a man be born of water and of the Spirit, he can not enter into the kingdom of God. That which is born of flesh is flesh; and that which is born of Spirit is spirit." After one has decided to accept Jesus Christ as Lord and Savior, this relationship can be cultivated and strengthened by that individual's willingness to submit to the will of God and seek his divine guidance for his or her individual life. This can be facilitated by an honest and systematic study of the scriptures, meditation, and prayer and fasting.

Through regular study of the word, God will open our under-standing as our knowledge of the scriptures grows. Also the setting aside of regular quiet, quality time to commune with God in prayer and meditation is essential to developing an intimate relationship with Him. During these times, all the cares of daily living should be totally blocked out of our minds so that we may focus our undivided attention on God. It is in these quiet still moments of prayer and meditation that God will often speak to us.

It is through this kind of honest and genuine sincerity of heart and mind, this reaching out, this soulful yearning to connect with god and understand who and what he really is, that God can reveal

282

Himself to us. This is what Christ meant in Matthew 6: 30-34: when he said, "But seek ye first the kingdom of God, and his righteousness; and all these things shall be added unto you." When we decide to make a genuine effort to study, fast, pray and meditate, God can commune with us. This is also what Jesus promised when He said, "Behold I stand at the door and knock. If any man hear my voice and open His heart, I will come in and sup with him and He with me." Rev. 3:20-22: The sincere acceptance of Jesus Christ as Lord and Savior and the receiving of his Holy Spirit, will create a hunger and thirst for the subsequent systematic study of the scriptures. This resulting growth in knowledge and grace will inevitably bring about a profound change in ones personality and point of view. If the study is honest and the heart sincere, such a profound transformation is inevitable. As a result, an individual's point of view moves from a primary focus on self to the point where the primary focus is on God. Consequently, one can clearly understand Paul's advice when He said, " be ye transformed by the renewing of your mind." Rom. 12:2 says, "And be not conformed to this world; but be ye transformed by the renewing of your mind, that ye may prove what is that good, and acceptable, and perfect, will of God." There is a preponderance of evidence that corroborates the fact that whatever one becomes immersed in he or she invariably becomes a part of.

Therefore, Jesus Christ promised that he who hungers and thirsts after righteousness, shall be filled. Matt. 5: 6. Fasting has been a tremendously effective way to develop discipline, self-control, and gain that all important inner strength which enables one to move into the spiritual realm. Therefore, it is extremely important to fast periodically. However, all of these activities must be engaged in with the utmost sincerity, sobriety, and most of all consistency. These things must be done in order to truly combine Christian theory with actual practice. In other words, it is to make certain that one talk coincides with his or her daily walk. There are far too many folk professing to be Disciples of Christ with their lips but their hearts are far from Him. They are just like the pimp, punk, and pusher preachers along with a host of other reprobates in the church who only perpetrate the rankest kind of spiritual fraud and are glaring examples of pathetic hypocrisy. This is what has made the African-American church weak, impotent, and all but completely irrelevant in the community.

Finally, I must reiterate the importance of and the imperative that one must clearly understand the difference between the practice of religious ritual and the higher practice of spirituality. In other words, having a true intimate relationship with Christ by allowing his spirit to connect with your own and letting His divine will become the central focus of your life, is the only thing that can possibly make you a true disciple of Jesus Christ. As a result Christ's divine will through his spirit living in you, inevitably becomes your own. That is if you are honestly willing to submit to him and truly make Him the Lord of your life. However, it is totally impossible to actually keep God's commandments and be a true disciple of Jesus Christ without His indwelling Holy Spirit. It is His Holy Spirit that makes one truly alive in Christ and endows the soul with the power to transcend carnality and the base desires of the flesh. This is why the primary focus of the church should be to lead people into the knowledge of the true historical and spiritually valid Christ. Instead there has been so much concentration on tradition, religious ritual, and observance of denominational dogma, that the primary imperative, has been virtually obscured. Jesus in His parable about the Good Samaritan poignantly underscored the difference between true spirituality and religiosity. This parable can be found in Luke Chapter 10, verses 25-37. Christ painted a vivid picture of spirituality and the lack of it in the soul of each individual as he encountered the wounded man on the road.

The Priest represented the religious establishment and his behavior clearly demonstrated that the practice of religion does not necessarily mean that one has a relationship with God. Furthermore, he showed by the Levite's behavior of seeing the wounded man, and not stopping to help, just how spiritually dead the Levite was. Then along came the Good Samaritan who was the only one of the three that actually looked upon the wounded man as God would have looked upon him. Consequently, he did the right thing, by showing mercy and tending to the man's needs. This, in my opinion is perhaps one of the most powerful and deeply revealing parables in the whole Bible concerning the fundamental difference between religiosity and spirituality. It clearly illustrates how one can be so devoutly religious and not spiritual at all. It clearly drives home the point that God is concerned with how we behave and the content of our character, and not merely what we profess to be to the outside world. He judges us according to who we really are, not what we merely profess to be. This is why He said, in John 14: 15: "If ye love me, then keep my commandments." This is why Jesus said, "If you love me then you will keep my commandments." He also declared, in John 2: 4: "He that saith, I know him and keepeth not his commandments, is a liar, and the truth is not in him."

Therefore, the mere practice and observance of religious ritual must not, and cannot automatically mean spirituality. Of course, the practice of religious ritual can be a stepping stone to true spirituality but it is only a vehicle for the possible attainment of such. Without a true relationship with God the practice of religion is nothing more than just the regular observance of ritual, the result is nothing more than a purely social and psychological experience. Consequently, this is why people can be fixtures in the church for years but without any significant change in behavior. Moreover, in their slavish devotion to religious ritual, they become dogmatic, self- righteous, and totally deluded with regard to an honest perception of themselves. They have become so self-righteous, outward looking, and super critical of others, that they are totally oblivious to their own faults. This is why many so-called, "Christians", can do all manner of wickedness and have not the slightest sense of shame or guilt. However they are expert in pointing out the slightest transgression or hint of wrong in the lives of others who also profess to be Christians. These kinds of religious reprobates are the scourge of the church and primarily responsible for the Church being in such a sorry state. Jesus said these kind of people have a form of Godliness but deny the power thereof. II Tim. 3: 5.

They also are vehement in professing Christ with their mouths but their hearts are far from him. He has warned that people such as these will not inherit the kingdom of heaven.

So, an honest study of the scriptures should inspire, encourage, and compel one to seek ye first, the kingdom of heaven and its righteousness, then all other things will be added unto you. This places a personal relationship with God at the top of the list, and makes it the primary requirement for true Christian discipleship. Therefore, this intimate relationship is the necessary and sufficient condition for truly being a part of Him. This is why Jesus said , "I am the true vine and he who abides in me, I will abide in him." John 15: 5. Therefore, one must be a part of Christ, in order to belong to Him. This truly intimate relationship with Christ can only be attained, cultivated, and strengthen by the honest and sincere willingness to accept and obey him. This means the road that most people take to find Christ is indeed in the church, but the mere practice of religious ritual does not necessarily mean that they will find Him there. Going to church, can indeed be a beginning, but one must go farther and deeper into the spiritual knowledge of Jesus Christ. The scripture declares, in Romans 10:9-10: "That" if thou shalt confess with thy mouth the Lord Jesus, and shalt believe in thy heart that God hath raised him from the dead, thou shalt be saved. For with the heart man believeth unto righteousness; and with the mouth confession is made unto salvation." One must first accept him as Lord and Savior and believe in his heart that God has raised him from the dead. Then this knowledge of Jesus Christ must lead to an inti-

287

mate relationship with Him. However, this intimate relationship with Christ can only be attained through sincere prayer, meditation, Study, fasting, and regular fellowshipping with other true Christians. These are the primary means to finding Christ and then understanding who and what he really is.

When you pray, you are talking to God, but when you meditate, you are allowing God to talk to you. So, in those sober moments of meditation and serene solitude, you will hear God talking to you. When you learn to meditate on God and allow Him to instruct and direct you, the consequences will be awesome in your life. For God has promised that, "He who keepeth his mind stayed on me, I will keep him in perfect peace." Isaiah 26,:3. You will began to feel and see the magnificent transformation in your own life and people around you will see it too. Then you will understand and truly appreciate the power of God to do for His people, just what He claims in His Word. The fruit of the spirit will begin to bloom and blossom abundantly in your life as the love of God is made manifest in your soul. As a result of his Holy Spirit living in your Soul, and your intimate relationship with him, you will inevitably become more and more like Him. For this is the goal of true Christian discipleship. When one is willing and able to reach out and accept Jesus Christ, and establish a truly intimate relationship with Him by allowing His spirit to dwell within the heart, he or she will indeed become a new creature.

These are the necessary and sufficient conditions which must be met before any one can ever hope to live a Holy and righteous life on this earth, or have the power and grace to do God's divine work on this earth. Therefore, true Christian discipleship can only be possible as a consequence of an intimate relationship with Christ attained by the presence of his Holy Spirit living in one soul. Anything else is but an exercise in futility and the cruelest delusion. For Jesus Christ declared in his word, "I am the way, the truth and the light." John 14 : 6.

Finally, any morally challenging or intellectually provocative ideas that I have set forth to greater illuminate the true meaning of Christian discipleship and the message of the gospel of Jesus Christ, I attribute to the eternal wisdom of the divine spirit of Christ living within me. However, any logical weaknesses or failures of literary lucidity found in this work, are totally my own. I have endeavored in this book, to deal with the raw, unvarnished, and unadulterated truth about Jesus Christ and the black church in a logical, rational, and most importantly spiritual way. Furthermore, in the context of this eternal and divine truth, I have endeavored to illuminate and elucidate the naked reality regarding the pathetic moral and spiritual condition of the black church. I have also discussed some reasons for the dismal failure of the great majority of its leadership as spiritual custodian and moral steward of the black community. However, this book is not at all, a blanket indictment of the black Church or the entire black clergy.

Clearly, there are some honest and sincere leaders in the church whom I believe, have been called by God, and qualified by him, to do his divine will. Consequently, their spiritual fruit speaks for itself.

Unfortunately, these individuals are few and far between. These Shepherds of God's sheep are known by their fruit, and it is because of their fruit that they have been legitimized and justified in the sight of god and those true Christians who have his indwelling spirit. On the contrary, I have been primarily referring throughout this book, to those shuffling, shamming, hopeless, handkerchief-head hypocrites who know in their secret hearts, that they are nothing but vicious wolves dressed in sheep clothes. So, you too, are known by your rotten fruit, and it is precisely your spiritually corrupt and morally putrid fruit that is threatening to spoil the entire black church harvest.

GLOSSARY

Abhor: 1.to regard with extreme repugnance or aversion; detest; loathe.

Acquiesce: 1. to submit or comply quietly or without protest.

Alienate: 1.to turn away the affection of; make indifferent or hostile: he has alienated all of his friends

Annals: 1.a record of events, especially a yearly record, usually in chronological order 2.a historical record.

Apartheid: 1.rigid policy of segregation of the nonwhite population. 2.any legal system or cultural practice that separates people according to their race or caste

Arbitrary: 1.subject to individual will or judgment without restriction; contingent solely upon one discretion: an arbitrary decision. 2.capricious; unreasonable; unsupported: an arbitrary demand for payment.

Antithesis: 1.opposition; contrast: the antithesis of right and wrong. 2.the exact opposite: her behavior was the antithesis of cowardly.

Audacity: 1.boldness or daring, especially with confident disregard for personal safety, conventional thought or other restrictions; nerve. 2.effrontery or arrogant disregard for insolence; shameless boldness.

Baleful: 1.menacing or malign, threatening evil: baleful glances.

Barbarity: 1.brutal or inhuman conduct; unmitigated cruelty. 2.ruthlessly wicked or mercilessly harsh or cruel.

Beguile: 1.to influence by guile; mislead; delude. 2. to take away from by cheating or deceiving; to be beguiled of your money.

Bestiality: 1.indulgence in beastlike appetites. 2.sexual relations between human beings and lower animals.

Bourgeoisie: 1.people who are generally materialistic and obsessed with mimicking respectability and convention. 2.characterized by or concerned with materialism and convention.

Bulwark: 1.any protection against external danger, injury, or annoyance. 2.any person or thing giving strong support in time of need, danger, or doubt.

Capricious: 1.subject to, lead by, or indicative of caprice or whim; erratic; mercurial.

Circumscribe: 1.to constrict the range or activity. 2. to draw a line around, define; restrict; delimit.

Concoct: 1.to devise or contrive: to concoct an excuse

Circumspect: 1. watchful and discreet; cautious; prudent: circumspect behavior.

Condescending: 1. to behave as if one is descending from a superior position, rank, or dignity. 2.showing condescension; implying a descent from dignity or superiority; patronizing.

Conspicuous: 1.easily seen or noticed; readily observable. 2.attracting special attention, as by outstanding qualities or eccentricities, striking.

Culture: 1.the sum total of ways of living built by a particular group of human beings and transmitted from one generation to another. 2.the beliefs and behaviors characteristic of particular social, ethnic, or age group; youth culture; the drug culture.

Cordwood: 1.a unit of volume used chiefly for fuel wood, generally equal to 128 cubic feet (3.6 cubic meters), usually specified as 8ft. 2.wood stacked in cords for use as fuel.

Debilitating: 1.to impair the health or strength of, weaken, disable, enfeeble or undermine.

Debauchery: 1.excessive indulgence in sensual pleasures; intemperance.

Debilitating: 1.to impair the health or strength of, weaken, disable, enfeeble or undermine

Decimate: 1 to destroy a great number or proportion of: the Civil War decimated the civilian population

Dehumanize: 1.to deprive of human qualities or attributes; divest of individuality.

Deleterious: 1.injurious to health. 2.harmful dangerous, or injurious to health.

Delineate: 1.to portray in words; describe with precision.

Delusion: 1.a false belief or opinion: delusions of grandeur. 2. a false belief that is resistant to reason or actual confrontation with fact: a paranoid delusion.

Diabolical: 1.devilish; fiendish; outrageously wicked: a diabolical plot.

Discrepancy: 1.an instance of difference or inconsistency.

Disjointed: 1.disconnected, incoherent: a disjointed discourse.

Dogma: 1. a system of principles or tenets, as of a church. 2. a specific tenet or doctrine authoritatively put fourth, as by a church.

Dogmatic: 1.of the nature of a dogma, doctrinal. 2.asserting opinions in a dictatorial manner, opinionated.

Duplicity: 1.deceitfulness in speech or conduct; double-dealing.

Dysfunctional: 1.impairment of function or malfunctioning, as of an organ or structure of the body. 2.a consequence of a social activity or structure that undermines a social system.

Eccentricity: 1.an oddity or peculiarity, as of conduct; weird: he has very strange or eccentric behavior.

Egomaniacal: 1.psychological abnormal egotism; extreme egocentrism.

Elucidate: 1.to make lucid or clear; explain.

Emanate: 1.to flow out, issue fourth; originate. 2.to send fourth: emit.

Emphatic: 1.clearly or boldly outlined. 2.forceful; insistent.

Endemic: 1.natural to or characteristic of a particular place, people, etc.: an endemic disease; endemic unemployment. 2.belonging exclusively or confined to a particular place: a species of bat endemic to Mexico.

Equilibrium: 1.a state of intellectual or emotional balance. 2. a state of balance between opposing forces or actions.

Estrange: to alienate the feelings or affections of; make unfriendly or hostile. 2.to remove to or keep at a distance.

Ethics: 1.a system or set of moral principles. 2.the proper rules of conduct recognized in respect to a particular set of human actions or governing a particular group, culture, etc.: medical ethics.

Ethnic: 1.pertaining to or characteristic of a people, especially a group (Ethnic Group) sharing a common and distinctive culture, religion, and language; African-Americans; Mexican-Americans; Chinese-Americans; Japanese-Americans. Obsession: 1.the domination of one thoughts and feelings by a persistent idea, image, desire, etc.

Ethnocentric: 1.the belief in the inherent superiority of one own ethnic group or culture. 2. a tendency to view alien groups or cultures from the perspective of one own.

Excommunicate: 1.to cut off from communion or membership, especially from the sacraments and fellowship of the church by ecclesiastical sentence. ..

Excoriate: 1. to denounce or berate severely; flay verbally: he was excoriated for his mistakes.

Exploitation: 1.the use or working of others, especially for profit: the institution of the Trans-Atlantic Slave Trade. 2.the use or manipulation of others for one own advantage.

Facsimile: 1.an exact copy, as of a book, painting, or manuscript.

Fathom: to penetrate to the truth of; to comprehend; understand: to fathom someone's motives.

Fiend: 1.devil: demon. 2. an extremely wicked or cruel person.

Fiefdom: 1.the state or domain of a feudal lord. 2. anything owned or controlled by one dominant person or group.

Frankenstein: 1. a monstrous creation that usually ruins its originator. 2. a monster in the shape of a man.

Functionary: 1.a person who works in a specified capacity, especially in government service; an official: civil servants and other functionaries.

Gaudy: 1.showy in a tasteless way; flashy: tawdry. 2.ostentatiously ornamented; garish.

Geld: 1. to castrate: to geld a stallion. 2. to deprive of something essential: to be gelded of one pried.

Genocide: 1.the deliberate and systematic extermination of a national, political, racial, or cultural group.

Hallucinogen: 1. a substance that produces hallucinations.

Heinous: 1.hateful. 2.hatefully or shockingly evil.

Hideous: 1.offensive to one of the senses, ugly. 2. morally offensive, shocking.

Holocaust: 1.any reckless destruction of human life: the Trans-Atlantic Slave Trade that lasted for more than four centuries. 2. (the Holocaust) the systematic mass slaughter of European Jews in Nazi concentration camps during World War II.

Horrendous: 1.dreadful, horrible.

Horrific: 1. an overwhelming and painful feeling caused by something shocking, terrifying, or revolting; a shuddering fear: to shrink back in horror.

Hypocrisy: 1.the false profession of desirable or publicly approved qualities, beliefs, or feelings, especially a pretense of having virtues, moral principles, or religious beliefs that one does not really possess.

Idiosyncrasy: 1.a characteristic, habit, mannerism, etc., that is peculiar to or distinctive of an individual. 2. a peculiarity of the physical or mental constitution, especially an aversion or deep sensitivity to certain foods or drugs.

Imperative: 1.absolutely necessary or required: it is imperative that we leave. 2.an order or command, an unavoidable obligation or requirement: the imperatives of leadership.

Indelible: 1. making marks that cannot be removed: indelible pens. 2. not removable, as by washing or erasure: indelible stains.

Indoctrination: 1. to instruct in a doctrine or ideology, especially dogmatically. 2. to teach, train, or inculcate; to imbue with a particular type of learning.

Inexpiable: not to be expiated; not allowing for expiation or atonement; an inexpiable crime. 2. incapable of being appeased; implacable: inexpiable hate.

Inexorable: unyielding; unalterable. 2. not to be persuaded, moved, or affected by prayers or entreaties; merciless.

Inferiorized: 1.low or lower in station, rank, degree, or grade. 2.of comparatively low grade; poor in quality; substandard.

Ingratiate: 1.to establish (oneself) in favor or the good graces of others, by deliberate effort.

Innate: 1.existing in one from birth; inborn; native: innate talents. 2.inherent in the character of something: an innate defect in the hypothesis.

Insatiable: 1.not satiable; incapable of being satisfied: insatiable hunger; insatiable ambition.

Insidious: 1.intended to entrap or beguile; an insidious plan. 2.stealthily treacherous or deceitful: an insidious enemy: double-dealing.

Institution: 1.an organization or establishment devoted to the promotion of a cause or program, especially one of a public, education, or charitable character. 2. a well-established and structured pattern of behavior or of relationships that is accepted as a fundamental part of a culture: the institution of marriage.

Juxtaposed: 1. to place close together or side by side, especially for comparison or contrast

Lackey: 1.a servile follower; toady.

Machination: 1. a crafty scheme or maneuver; an intrigue.

Malevolent: 1.wishing evil or harm to others; malicious. 2.producing harm or evil; injurious.

Malignant: 1.very dangerous or harmful in influence or effect. 2. a tumor characterized by uncontrolled growth; cancerous, invasive, or metastatic.

Myth: 1.a traditional or legendary story, especially one that involves gods and heroes and explains a cultural practice or natural object or phenomenon. 2. a belief or set of beliefs, often unproven or false, that have accrued around a person, phenomenon, or institution: myths of racial superiority.

Moral: 1.of, pertaining to, or concerned with the principles of right conduct or the distinction between right and wrong; ethical: moral attitudes. 2.capable of recognizing and then conforming to the rules of right conduct: a moral being.

Mobilize: 1.to put into movement or circulation. 2.to assemble and make ready for movement.

Myriad: 1.consisting of a very great but indefinite number.

Narcissistic: 1.inordinate fascination with oneself; excessive self-love; vanity. 2.erotic gratification derived from admiration of one own physical or mental attributes.

Nuance: 1.a subtle difference or distinction, as in expression or meaning. 2. a slight difference or variation in color or tone.

Negro: 1.of, designating, or characteristic of the traditional racial divisions of humankind, generally marked by brown to black skin, thick lips, large noses, dark eyes, and woolly or crisp hair, and especially the indigenous peoples of sub-Saharan Africa. 2.a member of the peoples traditionally classified as the Negro race.

Nostalgically: 1. a wistful or sentimental longing for places, things, acquaintances, or conditions belonging to the past.

Ostentation: 1.pretentious or conspicuous display or deliberate behavior intended to impress others.

Ostensively: 1.clearly or manifestly demonstrative.

Obsequious: 1.characterized by or showing servile complaisance or deference; fawning; sycophantic: obsequious servants.

Obsolete: 1.no longer in general use; fallen into disuse: obsolete customs. 2.of a discarded or outmoded type; out-of-date: an obsolete battleship.

Paradoxically: 1.a seemingly contradictory or absurd statement that expresses a possible truth. 2. a person, thing, or situation exhibiting an apparently contradictory nature.

Phenomenon: 1.a fact, occurrence, or circumstance observed or observable: the phenomena of nature. 2.something that is remarkable or extraordinary.

Precept: 1.a commandment or direction given as a rule of action or conduct. 2.an injunction as to moral conduct; maxim.

Predicate: 1.to proclaim; declare; affirm; assert.

Paradigm: 1.an example serving as a model; pattern: a paradigm of virtue.

Parasitic: of, pertaining to, or characteristic of parasites: bloodsucking leeches.

Pathology: 1.the conditions and processes of a disease. 2.any deviation from a healthy, normal, or efficient condition.

Perverse: 1.turned away from what is right, good, or proper; extremely wicked or corrupt.

Pretentious: 1.making an exaggerated outward show; ostentatious; showy. 2.full of pretension; characterized by the false assumption of dignity, importance, or artistic distinction.

Pretext: 1.something put forward to conceal a true purpose or object; ostensible reason; excuse. 2.the misleading appearance or behavior assumed with this intention; subterfuge.

Progeny: 1.offspring collectively; children. 2.something that originates or results from something else; outcome; issue.

Protracted: 1.to prolong in time. 2.space, extend, lengthen, elongate, and stretch.

Pomposity: 1.an instance of being pompous, as by ostentatious loftiness of language or behavior; showy, pretentious, or brazen. 2.pompous flaunting of importance.

Quintessential: 1.the pure and concentrated essence of a substance. 2.the most perfect embodiment of something.

Putrescent: 1. decay, rot, becoming putrid; undergoing putrefaction. 2. of or pertaining to putrefaction.

Relegate: 1.to send or consign one, or an entire group, to an inferior position, places, or condition. 2.to send into exile; banish.

Relentless: 1.unyieldingly severe, strict, or harsh; unrelenting.

Regal: 1.of or pertaining to a king or queen; royal. 2.stately; splendid.

Revile: 1.to address or speak of with contemptuous, abusive, or opprobrious language.

Religious: 1.scrupulously faithful; conscientious: with religious care. 2.imbued with or exhibiting religion; pious; devout.

Scurrilous: 1.coarsely jesting: obscene vulgar

Superficial: 1.concerned with or comprehending only what is on the surface or obvious. 2.shallow; not profound or thorough.

Sycophantic: 1.a self-seeking, servile flatterer; fawning parasite.

Servile: 1.slavishly submissive or obsequious; fawning: servile flatterers. 2 characteristic of, proper to, or customary for slaves; abject: servile obedience.

Sanctimonious: 1.showing or marked by false piety or righteousness; hypocritically religious or virtuous.

Sadistic: 1.sexual gratification gained by causing pain or degradation to others. 2.pleasure in being cruel.

Subordinate: 1.placed in or belonging to a lower order or rank. 2.subject to or under the authority of a superior; subservient; dependent; inferior.

Scurvy: 1.a disease marked by swollen and bleeding gums livid spots on the skin, and prostration and caused by a lack of vitamin C. 2 a contemptible, despicable, or lowlife person.

Suasion: 1.the act of attempting to persuade: persuasion.

Superficial: 1.concerned with or comprehending only what is on the surface or obvious. 2.shallow; not profound or thorough.

Subjugate: 1.to bring under complete control or subjection; conquer; master. 2. to make submissive or subservient; enslave.

Syndrome: 1.a group of symptoms that together are characteristic of a specific disease, disorder, or the like. 2.a predictable, characteristic or pattern of behavior that tends to occur under certain circumstances: the empty nest syndrome.

Training: 1.the education, instruction, or discipline of a person or thing that is being trained. 2.the status or condition of a person that has been trained; soldiers in top training.

Translucent: 1.easily understandable; lucent. 2.clear; transparent: translucent seawater.

Unconscionable: 1.not restrained by conscience; unscrupulous. 2.excessive; extortionate.

Unmitigated: 1.not mitigated; not softened or lessened. 2.absolute or unqualified; an unmitigated madman.

Unilateral: 1.relating to, occurring on, or involving one side only. 2.undertaken or done by or on behalf of one side, party, or faction; not mutual: unilateral disarmament.

Unctuous: 1.characterized by affected earnestness or moralistic fervor; excessively suave or smug. 2.characteristic of an unguent or ointment; oily; greasy.

Vociferous: 1.crying out noisily. 2.characterized by noisy or vehement outcry: vociferous protests.

Vicariously: 1.felt or enjoyed through imagined participation in the experience of others: a vicarious thrill.

Vitriolic: 1.very caustic or bitter; scathing: a vitriolic denunciation.

White supremacy: a cultural belief that the white race is naturally or inherently superior to all other groups that it has classified as nonwhite on the planet: therefore this white collective has been divinely anointed to control and dominate the affairs of the globe.

"Random House Dictionary